SOLUTION-FOCUSED BRIEF THER

OXFORD WORKSHOP SERIES:

SCHOOL SOCIAL WORK ASSOCIATION OF AMERICA

Series Advisory Board

Judith Shine, President
Susan L. Ellis, Executive Director
Randy A. Fisher
Stephen P. Hydon
Donna J. Secor

Evidence-Based Practice in School Mental Health
James C. Raines

The Domains and Demands of School Social Work Practice
Michael S. Kelly

Solution-Focused Brief Therapy in Schools
Michael S. Kelly, Johnny S. Kim, and Cynthia Franklin

SOLUTION-FOCUSED BRIEF THERAPY IN SCHOOLS

A 360-Degree View of Research and Practice

Michael S. Kelly
Johnny S. Kim
Cynthia Franklin

OXFORD WORKSHOP SERIES

OXFORD
UNIVERSITY PRESS

2008

OXFORD
UNIVERSITY PRESS

Oxford University Press, Inc., publishes works that further
Oxford University's objective of excellence
in research, scholarship, and education.

Oxford New York
Auckland Cape Town Dar es Salaam Hong Kong Karachi
Kuala Lumpur Madrid Melbourne Mexico City Nairobi
New Delhi Shanghai Taipei Toronto

With offices in
Argentina Austria Brazil Chile Czech Republic France Greece
Guatemala Hungary Italy Japan Poland Portugal Singapore
South Korea Switzerland Thailand Turkey Ukraine Vietnam

Published by Oxford University Press, Inc.
198 Madison Avenue, New York, New York 10016

www.oup.com

Library of Congress Cataloging-in-Publication Data
Kelly, Michael S. (Michael Stokely), 1968–
Solution-focused brief therapy in schools: 360-degree view of
research and practice / Michael S. Kelly, Johnny S. Kim, Cynthia Franklin.
p. cm.—(Oxford workshop series: School Social Work
Association of America)
Includes bibliographical references and index.
ISBN 978-0-19-536629-7
1. Educational counseling—United States. 2. Solution-focused brief therapy—United States.
3. School social work—United States. I. Kim, Johnny S. II. Franklin, Cynthia. III. Title.
LB1027.5.K435 2008
371.4'6—dc22   2007052832

1 3 5 7 9 8 6 4 2

Printed in the United States of America
on acid-free paper

Contents

SOLUTION-FOCUSED BRIEF THERAPY IN SCHOOLS

I

∎∎∎

Introduction: A 360-Degree View of Solution-Focused Brief Therapy (SFBT) in Schools

Since its creation in the 1980s, solution-focused brief therapy (SFBT) has gradually become a common and accepted treatment option for many mental health professionals (MacDonald, 2007). With its emphasis on client strengths and short-term treatment, SFBT would appear to be well suited to school mental health contexts, given the wide array of problems presenting in school settings and the large caseloads of most school social workers (Franklin, Biever, Moore, Clemons, & Scamardo, 2001; Newsome, 2005). This book, as part of the Oxford Workshop Series, will present a "360-degree" view of SFBT in school settings from meta-analytic, intervention research, and practice perspectives.

The chapters in this book will take you through a 360-degree view of SFBT in school social work practice. You will first learn about SFBT itself, from its earliest beginnings in the 1980s to the present day (Chapter 2). In Chapter 2 special emphasis will be placed on the ways in which the SFBT techniques can be applied directly to school social work practice realities. In Chapter 3, the question, "does SFBT really work?" will be given a thorough review, with results from a recent meta-analysis on SFBT practice and other research on the approach giving a full picture of the current state of the science in regards to SFBT practice. Chapter 4 will feature a particularly exciting new approach to using SFBT in schools, the WOWW program ("Working On What Works"). WOWW is a teacher coaching intervention designed to increase teacher-student collaboration for better learning environments, and along with a detailed description of the authors' WOWW intervention program currently underway in Chicago, the promising outcome data from the initial WOWW program will be analyzed and discussed.

Another exciting phenomenon underway in several schools internationally is the adoption of SFBT ideas and principles throughout the entire school curriculum and discipline process. These "solution-focused schools," although still small in number, have a lot to teach us about ways we can make our own schools more solution focused. In Chapter 5, we focus on one such school that the authors have consulted with extensively, Garza School in Austin, Texas. Chapter 6 draws on some of the positive outcomes of the Garza experience to show how other school social workers in a diverse array of K-12 school environments have translated SFBT ideas into their own contexts. Other than Chapter 2, this will be the "how-to" chapter of the book, with special focus on equipping you to begin doing SFBT-based school interventions as soon as possible. Finally, because SFBT is only 25 years old, we thought it appropriate to ask expert SFBT researchers and practitioners to help us project ahead what the next 25 years might hold for SFBT in school settings (Chapter 7).

This book is divided into sections within each chapter to allow you to access information easily and use it to apply SFBT ideas to your school practice. The sections are as follows (*Note*: some of our book chapters will have more on one section than another, depending on the topics being covered in these chapters):

> **The history:** This section will provide the background information on the specific area of SFBT being discussed in the chapter.
> **The research**: This section explains what the best and most current evidence has to say.
> **The skills**: This section provides specific SFBT skills needed for the concepts discussed in the chapter.
> **The application**: Using case studies and other tools, each chapter will show you how to implement the techniques and ideas discussed in the chapter.
> **The future**: In this section, we will share the information on current trends in SFBT research and practice, as well as challenges and controversies that are alive in the field.

In Schools, Solutions Are Everywhere

Problems abound in school settings. Students aren't always ready to learn, teachers aren't always sure how to deal with the underachieving and/or defiant student and instead claim that he/she just "doesn't care," and parents are at times eager to find someone from the school to blame. Into these loaded situations, the overall school climate provides possible additional stresses, with school violence, bullying, gang activity, and other illicit behavior happening on school grounds while school administrators try to maintain "zero tolerance" for these behaviors on the one hand, and on the other, try hard to foster a positive, child-centered learning environment to increase academic achievement for all students. And as if all these problems weren't enough, the field of education is under pressure from federal, state, and local governments to provide accurate and measurable progress toward yearly goals, a process that has only become more pronounced since the implementation of the No Child Left Behind legislation in 2002.

But solutions also abound in school settings. Second graders wake up early and tell their parents that they can't wait to get to school to see their teachers and their friends. Teachers stop in the hallway outside their class to tell colleagues about a new project they're excited about embarking on with their students. In cafes, beauty shops, and church basements, parents encourage other parents to send their own kids to their child's school because of all the great things it has going for it. School leaders, in collaboration with local law enforcement, parents, and the students themselves, create zones of safety even for children living in economically distressed and dangerous neighborhoods. All the school stakeholders (teachers, parents, kids, and administrators) welcome higher accountability standards and frame them as an opportunity to foster a more collaborative and high-achieving academic culture.

Schools can be places of solutions, strengths, and successes. There are numerous practical ways for school-based mental health professionals (school social workers, school counselors, and school psychologists) to harness the solutions that are already happening in their schools.

If SFBT was "born" in the 1980s, as we will describe in more detail in Chapter 2, it could be said to be in an early stage of adolescence now: mature enough to stand on its own for some things but not able to claim and prove that it can do everything it wants to. A recent database search revealed that there are 50 books in print on SFBT, SFBT associations in over 10 countries, and several annual national and international conferences devoted to SFBT that have been convened. In Chapter 3, we will share findings from a meta-analysis of SFBT studies that show that there are solid (though modest) impacts from the current SFBT practice literature. In comparison to a more heavily researched approach such as cognitive-behavioral therapy (CBT), SFBT hasn't yet been able to claim the volume of studies that demonstrate its effectiveness, but as we shall show in Chapter 3, it is on its way to joining CBT as a practice that has shown some empirical efficacy (Kim, 2008).

We are sharing a 360-degree view of an approach that is actually at a stage of a work in progress, to which additional empirical research, theory, and practical applications are being added each year. In the spirit of evidence-based practice transparency, we won't overstate or play down the available research on SFBT's effectiveness: we will share these findings with you and let you join us in assessing how well these findings will apply to your own practice style and school context.

Why SFBT Is Well Suited to School Social Work Practice

Problems and solutions, to the thinking of a SFBT school social worker, are always "abounding" in any school context. Indeed, as we shall see in this book, one of the more liberating notions of SFBT is that change is always happening, and requires our attention to be focused on the small changes that are making potentially large differences in the lives of our clients. What we do with those small, sometimes hard-to-see changes is what make us SFBT school social workers, and it could even make our school contexts move toward becoming more solution focused in their approaches to the key educational issues of today.

The Case of Bonita:
Little Changes Now = Big Changes Later

Bonita was one of the first students I met at my first-ever school social work position. She was lost, literally. She had just come to the school as a sixth grader and wasn't sure where her self-contained special education class was. She asked me for directions and I introduced her to her teacher. The next week, she was in my office, crying about how much she missed her old school and didn't like the older kids at our junior high. She had announced to her teacher, "I hate this school and I'm staying at home tomorrow!" While I validated her feelings of sadness and anxiety, I asked her to tell me if she had noticed anything getting better for her at our school. She said that she still had a good friend from her old school with her, and that they were in the same class together. I asked her to tell me how she would rank her experience at our school so far on a scale of 1 to 10, with 10 being the highest in the scale. She asked through her tears, "can you go lower than 1?!" I said, "sure," and she said, "It's a 0."

I asked her what would it take for her to get her to say that being at our school deserved a score of 2 or a 3, and she said, "a total miracle." I then asked her to imagine that just such a miracle had happened that night and the next day she when was at our school and everything was better for her here. In such a case, what would be the first thing she'd notice was different? Bonita thought for a while and replied: "I would be able to open my locker by myself."

It turned out that Bonita had never used a combination lock before and this had made her very anxious, as well as making her feel inadequate because all the other kids in her class were already doing it without problems. We set a goal of working on her locker combination skills with her teacher, and within weeks Bonita was smiling and laughing each morning as I watched her walk into school.

This short case example demonstrates how the possibilities for change are indeed "everywhere" and skilled SFBT school social workers can harness change to help a client make big changes in their everyday school behavior. Read the example not only to know about the specific SFBT techniques in action (more on those later), but also to understand how the different members of the client system perceive the intervention being conducted by the solution-focused school social worker and then collaborate with the social worker to help students succeed.

Like Bonita in our first case example, schools themselves are going through their own transition in relation to the utilization of mental health services. Some policy makers and educational leaders call for schools to become "full-service operations," providing students and their parents with the mental health, vocational, and English-language training that aren't adequately provided by external community agencies. Still others claim that school-based mental health is an "extra" service that is supportable only to the degree that it produces demonstrable differences in student academic achievement and thus allows students to successfully compete in the global economy. One of our colleagues remembers being told by a local superintendent that he would support our colleagues' SFBT research project only if it made a measurable positive impact on "bottom-line" education issues for his K-8 district (in his case, this meant higher GPAs and increased attendance).

School leaders and parents are right in wanting more from school-based mental health services, and the profession itself has only begun to recognize the need to be more transparent with community stakeholders about the relative effectiveness of the interventions we typically employ in our school practices. What this book will do is to equip you with a solid working knowledge in the ideas and techniques behind SFBT, acquaint you with the most current evidence on the overall effectiveness research on SFBT, and finally demonstrate several examples of school social workers making SFBT happen in their particular school contexts. It is our hope that by taking a look at SFBT from a 360-degree perspective, you will be ready to bring more specific SFBT ideas and techniques into your school in the coming years.

Advantages of SFBT in a School Setting

SFBT Is Strengths Based

SFBT is an approach that posits that people have strengths; moreover, SFBT says that those strengths are active, *right now*, in helping clients manage

---

BOX 1.1 Advantages of SFBT

- SFBT is strengths based
- SFBT is client centered
- In SFBT, small changes matter
- SFBT is portable
- SFBT is adaptable
- SFBT can be as brief (or as long) as you want it to be
- SFBT enables practitioners to gain cultural competence
- SFBT can be adapted to special education IEP goals

---

their situation. The issue isn't that clients can't solve their problem without additional training or somehow submitting to the school social workers' view of the problem: rather, it's their own inherent strengths that will ultimately be what they use to resolve their problems. Why does this approach help in a school setting? Students, teachers, and parents are likely going to be visible to the school social worker even when they're not being "treated." In addition to using actual SFBT techniques to access strengths in clients, school social workers have a unique opportunity to observe their school clients handling a variety of other challenges in their day-to-day contact with the school population. By not presuming that all clients are inherently in need of some treatment for a particular pathology or dysfunction, strengths-based school social workers are free to see their clients do a variety of things well and even figure out how to ask questions that help their client mobilize those inherent strengths to do something about the particular problem they are seeing the school social worker for. In addition, school social workers usually have to document their work with clients by writing reports and case summaries: SFBT gives them ample opportunities to focus on their client's strengths and incorporate those strengths into their written assessments and other paperwork.

SFBT Is Client Centered

SFBT starts from where the client is at in sometimes dramatic and powerful ways, creating contexts where clients can determine their own goals and make decisions about how and where they wish to make changes in their lives. In school settings, whether it is a student or a teacher, a solution-oriented school social worker may be more likely to notice and respond to what clients are actually asking for and wishing to change. In addition to increasing the likelihood that the clients will implement the particular intervention and maintain progress toward their goals, focusing on what the clients want to change also presents the possibility of making the whole referral and placement process in school settings more client focused and thus (hopefully) more effective than standard behavior modification plans that might not always include the specific goals and wishes of every part of the client system.

In SFBT, Small Changes Matter

One of the biggest challenges in school social work practice is the common complaint heard from parents, administrators, and teachers that change

---

brought about for a particular student's emotional/behavioral problems is slow or too "small." SFBT stands this thinking on its head and calls on school social workers to focus on helping clients make small changes and maintain these changes, with the theory being that with those small successes in hand, the clients will begin to see themselves as more capable of making larger changes in their lives. Again and again, we have seen this principle play out with students in our school social work practice; by making one part of a problem go away, or by helping a teacher see one strength of a student that they had "given up on," larger changes became possible and the clients went ahead and made them with minimal coaching or encouragement on our part.

SFBT Is Portable

Though SFBT started as and remains a set of techniques rooted in clinical psychotherapy practice, there are numerous other nonclinical school settings where SFBT can make a difference. Almost anywhere in a school is a potential site for applying SFBT techniques or ideas: the class meeting where students are asked to scale their own behavior and talk about what would have happened differently if they rated themselves higher the next week; the special education staffing where parents and teachers are asked to describe exceptions where the student doesn't display a problem behavior in an effort to learn about what things the learning environment (as well as the student) might do differently to avoid repeating the problem behavior; or the playground mediation where students are asked to think about how doing one thing differently might make a difference to a conflict they're having. All these examples (and many more that you will read about in this book) underline the diverse ways in which school social workers can bring SFBT into their diverse settings and adapt SFBT ideas to their multiple roles within their schools.

SFBT Is Adaptable

SFBT can be folded or nested into other techniques being used by SFBT clinicians. Most experienced school social workers we've worked with have characterized their practice approach as "eclectic." One of the best features of SFBT as a maturing practice approach is its ability to be integrated into other practice approaches. Clearly, there are elements of SFBT that fit nicely within a cognitive or behavior treatment framework. Even practitioners who tend to favor approaches that are based more on discovering how the past impacts a student's current functioning will appreciate the aspects of SFBT where clients are asked to set goals for their progress and to gauge how well they're doing based on scaling questions.

SFBT Can Be as Brief (Or as Long) as You Want It to Be

One of the frequent complaints we hear about SFBT is that it is too surface oriented and too brief to get into the "real work." This may have been a fair criticism of SFBT in its early stages (which deliberately defined itself as being opposed to long-term treatment), but now it is clear that SFBT is easily adapted to single-session, brief, and long-term treatment processes. The nature of SFBT (the thinking that change is possible and constant) does not mean that clients who have more long-term treatment plans (such as those students in schools who have individualized education plans [IEPs] requiring a year of social work services) can't benefit from the strength-based approach inherent to SFBT. In our practice experience, some students who we saw on a long-term basis wound up having several distinct solution-focused brief therapies over the course of the year. The process of helping them was similar, but the issues changed as students learned how to manage one problem and then faced another new problem.

SFBT Enables Practitioners to Gain Cultural Competence

All school personnel (school social workers included) are realizing the increasing importance of cultural competence skills in helping them engage with and teach students from culturally diverse backgrounds. Several recent scholars have noted that one of the main persisting aspects of the racial "achievement gap" is the cultural competence gap that separates white educators from the students of color whom they are trying to empower and teach (Delpit & Kohl, 2006; Ferguson, 2002; Tripod Project, 2007). By emphasizing how clients perceive their problems and how they might devise solutions that fit their own preferences, SFBT appears to be well suited to help school social workers practice in a more culturally competent fashion. In addition, through the example of SFBT pioneers like Insoo Kim Berg, SFBT has always advocated that clinicians frequently adopt "one-down" positions that allow clients to be in charge of their treatment in ways that avoid the clients from perceiving the school social worker as pushy or domineering. Clinicians who are perceived as authoritarian or being interested only in their own particular approach to treatment are often labeled as cultur-ally insensitive by minorities who are receiving mental health treatment

(Fong, 2004; McGoldrick, Giordano, & Pearse, 1996; Wing Sue & McGoldrick, 2005), and SFBT clearly offers an alternative way for school social workers to engage clients in clinical work without making them feel forced to adopt the school social worker's worldview.

SFBT Can be Adapted to Special Education IEP Goals

For many school social workers, a lot of their services are delivered to students who have yearly goals for treatment, usually expressed through an IEP. SFBT, along with CBT, is well suited to helping school social workers write those goals and collaborate with their clients to meet those goals successfully. By identifying discrete changes and applying scaling questions, school social workers can easily integrate SFBT-thinking into their IEP goals. Though this is an area that has so far not been studied empirically, it is the authors' contention from their own school experience that the very process of creating IEP goals with students, teachers, and parents in a solution-focused manner has enhanced the eventual achievement of those goals by motivating the client system to move towards solutions rather than remaining stuck in only talking about the problem.

Summary

SFBT is well suited to school social work practice and school contexts. A solution-focused school social worker can help students, particularly those who are harder to reach, think about ways to focus on what's working and how they can change their lives in positive ways. SFBT, although not originally created for application in a school context, is clearly an adaptable, portable practice philosophy that, as we will see in next chapters, can be used in many diverse school contexts at multiple levels of intervention.

2

SFBT at 25: The Development of a Treatment Approach

In this chapter, we will highlight the contributions made by solution-focused brief therapy (SFBT) pioneers Insoo Kim Berg and Steve de Shazer, as well as other school-based SFBT practitioners and scholars. We focus on the main facets of the SFBT approach, specifically the way solution-focused practitioners think about change, client capacities, and the nature of client resistance. We will also contrast the techniques of SFBT with other well-known treatment approaches used in schools, such as cognitive-behavioral therapy (CBT) to show how SFBT differs from other approaches that school social workers are already using.

The History

In the late 1970s, psychotherapy in the United States was at its zenith. The evidence for this high point was everywhere: mental health services had gone mainstream, self-help books topped the best-seller lists, and perhaps most important, economic conditions had conspired to create a high degree of health insurance support for mental health services (Cushman, 1995; Moskowitz, 2001; Wylie, 1994). The insurance money for psychotherapy was usually not time limited and was generous, allowing therapists from psychiatry, psychology, and social work to earn six-figure incomes. A review of the popular and academic literature of that time reveals that there were three main schools of psychotherapy that were popular then: psychodynamic therapy, CBT, and humanistic psychology (Norcross & Goldried, 2003). Therapy was available, usually open ended or long term, to almost anyone who knew where to find it.

By the early 1990s, things had changed dramatically. Although self-help books continued to crowd American bookstore shelves, psychotherapy had become a profession that was largely dominated by managed care. Psychotherapy, although still readily available to many people who needed it, was time limited, and often restricted to no more than 20 sessions a year. Fees for therapists were capped as well, and the golden days of lucrative therapy practices had begun to fade (Duncan, Hubble, & Miller, 1999; Lipchik, 1994; Wylie, 1994). To a psychoanalytically informed practitioner used to seeing patients for a decade or more, this new era was dreary indeed.

Something else important happened in psychotherapy in this era, in the heart of America, in a city known more for bratwurst and beer than therapy innovation. In Milwaukee, Wisconsin, a group of therapists led by Insoo Kim Berg and Steve de Shazer started working with clients in radically different ways. They saw clients for a few sessions, often no more than five or six times. They asked questions that focused less on client problems and more on how clients had previously solved the problems they faced.

BOX 2.1 Difference Between Solution-Focused Brief Therapy (SFBT) and Conventional Treatment

SFBT SOCIAL WORKER MODELS	PROBLEM-FOCUSED SOCIAL WORKER
• What could be a small step toward achieving your goal?	• How does it make you feel when the problem occurs?
• What has been going well in your life?	• When does the problem occur in your life?
• What will you be doing differently when the problem is no longer present?	• What thoughts do you have when the problem occurs?
• How did you know that was the right thing to do?	• How do others react when you are behaving that way?

The focus was more on using solutions from the past to handle issues of the present and future. Although consciousness of client's experience of loss, trauma, and other difficult feelings was incorporated into their work, they were not focussed on the client's actual strengths and capacities to move beyond those difficult issues quickly (Berg, 1994; de Shazer, 1988).

Clients themselves were viewed as experts on their own problems. Rather than position psychotherapists as the figure of authority or as the expert in the clinical relationship, this new approach put the therapist in a different role, that of a curious questioner who asked a sequence of questions and offered suggestions that both brought out the client's strengths and set them on the path to finding their own solution, not the answer or solution that the school social worker had chosen for the client. Overall, the presumption of the therapists in Milwaukee was that clients could change, would change, and were actually changing already. These Milwaukee-based therapists were creating a new approach to therapy, a collection of techniques and activities that eventually became known as SFBT (Berg, 1994; De Jong & Berg, 2002; de Shazer, 1988; MacDonald, 2007). Box 2.1 shows some differences between SFBT and conventional treatment.

The Skills

As the SFBT Association makes clear, "(SFBT) should be characterized as a way of clinical thinking and interacting with clients more than a list of techniques (SFBTA, 2006, p. 2)." By viewing clients as being engaged in a constant process of change, solution-focused clinicians are poised to tap into the client's natural ways of healing and existing ways of viewing change (Tallman & Bohart, 1999).

The First Session: How SFBT Distinguishes Itself

SFBT is more of an approach than a set of sequential techniques that must be followed rigidly (SFBTA, 2006). Every client is different and every professional using SFBT is going to adapt his or her approach to the specific client's needs and developmental level. This is perhaps most evident in a school setting, where the client's age can range from 5 years (a kindergartner) to 65 years (a veteran principal). We focus here on how, in the first session, SFBT distinguishes itself from other treatment models by providing some examples on not only how to "start" doing SFBT but also to contextualize the different directions SFBT can take depending on the client's goals and frame of reference.

Presession Change, Exception Questions, and Other Key SFBT Concepts

One distinctive facet of the SFBT approach is the attention that the solution-focused school social worker pays to changes that are already in motion from the moment the first session was scheduled and the actual first meeting. This is called "presession change" and allows the solution-focused school social worker to model the SFBT concept that change is a natural and constant occurrence, and that this notion can become a source of hope and empowerment for clients as they struggle to change what initially seems to be overwhelming problems that they fear will take years of treatment to address (Berg, 1994; De Jong & Berg, 2001; Murphy, 1996; Selekman, 2005). To do this, solution-focused school social workers at the first meeting ask questions such as, "since we talked on the phone and scheduled this first meeting, have there been any changes in the way that you and your son are getting along at home?" or "since Mrs. Smith asked me to come and see you, has anything changed in the way you're behaving in her class?" On the basis of any changes that the client identifies, the solution-focused school professional moves on to amplify that change and see what ideas the client might have about maintaining that change into the future. Box 2.2 describes questions typically used in SFBT.

A hopeful, almost expectant tone pervades most initial SFBT sessions, where clients are welcomed and given the chance to describe how they are already changing before they've even begun treatment. In our practice experience, we have seen this approach resonate with students who are used to mental health professionals who start their first sessions trying to probe for underlying causes to the problem behavior by asking detailed questions about the student's history. By setting the context squarely in the present and asking clients to imagine a new future, we have seen many students embrace this perspective and tailor it to their own goals.

This approach to clients is immediately apparent through the ways that solution-focused clinicians talk to their clients from the first session. Solution-focused school social workers tend to focus on different areas in their initial contact with clients compared to typical treatment approaches that are more rooted in using the medical model to assess for client pathology. The questions tend to focus on what the clients see as their presenting problem, but little time is spent talking about root causes or past family history that might have contributed to the problem. Rather, from the first meeting, clients are encouraged to talk about their situation in present and future terms, with the expectation communicated that they are more in charge of their problem

BOX 2.2 Questions Typically Asked in Solution-Focused Brief Therapy (SFBT)

Coping Questions
- How do you keep from giving up since you have tried everything?
- How have you managed to cope so far?
- What keeps you hanging in there?
- What has been going well in your life?

Looking for Solutions
- What small change will you notice when things change?
- How would you know if our talk would make a big difference?
- What has been better for you this week?
- When didn't you have this problem? Even a little bit?

Moving Forward
- What will you do instead of cutting class to smoke?
- What will be a small sign that you are no longer depressed?
- What will you notice about yourself? What will others notice about you that is different?
- How could you do more of that this week?

now than they might have previously felt. In contrast to a first session, where great energy and effort is expended by both the school social worker and the client to describe the problem and all of its attendant impacts for the client, solution-focused school social workers tend to ask clients to tell them what they might have already tried in order to address the problem, and assuming that the client can't name anything that's worked, identify those times or situations where the problem isn't present (or at least isn't as problematic).

Clients are also encouraged to think of the future, even in the first session. This can be done through questions that orient the session toward future hopes, or more specifically, by asking them the "miracle question" or "scaling questions" that invite clients to imagine a future reality that they might be able to start bringing into being. For the miracle question, clients are asked to imagine that when they go to bed that night, a miracle takes place, and when they wake up, their problem is solved and they feel better and more hopeful about their day. The solution-focused school social worker then asks, "What would be the first thing that you would notice about your new situation that told you that the miracle had taken place?" This opens up the possibilities that clients can see changes happening in their lives and identify first steps at achieving more of the changes they want (Berg, 1994). Scaling questions can be used for a variety of subjects, asking clients to rate their ability to manage their problem on a scale of 1 to 5, with 1 being "not able to handle my problem at all" and 5 being "fully able to handle my problem." Assuming a client rates his or her problem as being at a 2, a solution-focused school social worker can ask the client what he or she would be doing differently if he or she was able to rate self at a "3" or "4" when they met the next week. With the scales, clients can be asked to imagine what they would need to do to raise (or lower, depending on the way the scale is framed) their score, and exceptions can be identified in their work where they may have already been doing things more in line with their goals.

Likewise, the focus on exception questions helps the client use the past pragmatically. By identifying times in the past when the problem wasn't affecting the client, or times when the client was more able to handle a similar situation successfully, the solution-focused school social worker invites the client to view his or her current reality as being less stuck and hopeless. It also encourages the client to imagine that the "exception" times could more easily become their future reality because as one client told us, "Hey, now that I realize that it's already been a problem I was able to beat before, why can't I do it again?"

Future Sessions and Goal Setting

Like many treatment approaches, SFBT favors the implementation of a goal-setting process between client and school social worker. Where SFBT differs is in the power sharing that goes on in setting these goals. Instead of a process where, over time, clients are expected to face their denial and accept a reality that the school social worker is advocating, the reality of the client is always paramount in the sessions (this produces some interesting contrasts and even conflicts when working in school settings with children referred by teachers, which we will discuss more fully in Chapter 7). Clients can change as much or as little as they want, and are given the freedom by the SFBT process to set goals that they can achieve. In some ways this goal-setting process mirrors some of what CBT school social workers do as they set treatment goals with clients on the basis of specific problematic thinking or behavior. The difference between CBT and SFBT here is that clients aren't required to adopt a particular approach to their behavior or adopt new ways of thinking about how their emotions are affected by their cognitions.

Compliments Count

Anyone watching a videotape of a practitioner doing SFBT will be immediately struck by how often the school social worker compliments the client over the course of a regular session (Berg, 1994). Because so much effort in SFBT is spent for identifying client resiliency and setting goals on the basis of strengths the clients have demonstrated in the past, it's understandable that clients begin to self-report the times between sessions that they have made at least small gains in solving their problems. Rather than take credit for helping the client make this change (or expressing frustration that the client isn't progressing more quickly), solution-focused school social workers are quick to highlight client gains and give them compliments about their progress.

These compliments aren't meant to be patronizing; good solution-focused school social workers know how to convey genuine pride and excitement at a client's progress, often saying things like, "that's great, tell me how you did that?" or "I am so impressed! What did you figure out to do that made you deal with your problem so successfully?" Clients take that feedback and are motivated to make more changes, either for the same problem or for a different problem that the solution-focused school social worker may not even be aware of yet (De Jong & Berg, 2002; Metcalf, 1995; Selekman, 2005).

Coping Questions

One persistent critique of SFBT has been that it is too optimistic and doesn't allow for clients to have deep emotional experiences in therapy (Lipchik, 1994; Nylund & Corsiglia, 1994). This has been acknowledged as a critique by SFBT founders (Miller & de Shazer, 2000), but in some ways, this strikes us as a straw man argument. If clients have strong upsetting emotional experiences in treatment, they are certainly encouraged by a solution-focused school social worker to experience those feelings, to cry, to yell, to express what they need to express. What SFBT does not do, and which confuses some people who are new to the approach, is place any inherent value on intense emotional experiences in therapy (Berg & Dolan, 2001; De Jong & Berg, 2001). Because SFBT presumes that clients can (and regularly do) solve their own problems, there is no particular weight given to any emotionally cathartic experience that might be triggered by the school social worker during sessions. Instead, great emphasis is placed on asking questions that allow clients to help the school social worker learn what the client wants to talk about, and how fast or slow they would like to go in exploring how to change their situation. In our two decades of doing solution-focused work in schools, we have witnessed many clients share their hopes and goals in SFBT with intense emotion; we have also seen many clients embrace the approach in a calm, somewhat playful way, with plenty of laughter and spontaneity punctuating the sessions. The focus has never been on the degree of emotional intensity; rather, it has always been on helping the client generate their own solutions (Berg, 1994; Miller & de Shazer, 2000).

The most concrete way to show how this approach works for chronic and seemingly debilitating problems that school clients deal with is the SFBT coping questions. Solution-focused school social workers often use these questions when a client is reporting significant difficulty and even some frustration that their situation hasn't gotten better. Questions like, "This situation sounds really hard—how have you managed to cope with it as well as you have thus far?" are designed to elicit client strengths and possible strategies that they may have used in the past to cope with their difficulties (Berg, 1994; Selekman, 2005). Another coping question that we've often used with students in this area when they are complaining about the seeming impossibility of their situations is, "How have you been able to keep this from even getting worse for you?" By framing the "impossible" situation as one that the student is able to still have some control over, the solution-focused school professional can explore what hidden capacities the student has for managing and potentially overcoming their problems.

Doing Something Different

One of the most exciting and fun aspects of doing SFBT in a school setting is the ability to try out new ideas and interventions with clients on the basis of their willingness to "do something different" about their problem. Rather than seek to teach clients to adopt a specific technique to handle their problems, such as possible problems associated with anger or difficulty in making friends, solution-focused school social workers explore what clients have done about the problem in the past and also what might be the new ideas they could try now. For example, an 11-year-old student we worked with was struggling with managing his temper in his classroom and hadn't found the traditional cognitive-behavioral anger management techniques offered by his special education teacher to be helpful. He told us that he had run out of ideas because everything he had tried before hadn't worked. When we told him that we thought it might be time to "do something different," he immediately warmed up to the idea and started brainstorming new ideas to tackle his anger problem. Being a young person, some of the ideas were admittedly wacky: no teacher was likely to let him play his GameBoy all day to fend off his tirades. However, after sifting through his ideas, the student settled on a creative solution that he was excited to implement and we thought his teacher would lend support to: he would work out with his teacher a list of "helper tasks" in the class that he would be able to do at any time he thought he was going to lose his temper. The teacher would get some help with things in the classroom, and the student would get to take his mind off his frustration and recharge.

Client Resistance? We Don't See It That Way . . .

The advantage of having concepts like coping questions, "doing something different," brainstorming, or exception questions when working with students is that it allows a solution-focused school social worker to quickly short-circuit student resistance to working on their problems. The very concept of resistance is eagerly debated in the SFBT literature (Berg, 1994; de Shazer, 1988; O'Hanlon & Bertolino, 1998), as most SFBT writers consider resistance to be more a product of the solution-focused professional's inability to find common ground with the clients than the clients' refusal to face their problems directly. By approaching the school client in a respectful, patient way, we have found that the ideas in SFBT have allowed us to find some workable goal for most clients in a school setting, and have allowed us to avoid labeling our clients as being "in denial" about their problems.

What SFBT Does (and Doesn't) Teach

Part of what has held back SFBT in some quarters is this notion that it doesn't "teach" anything new to a client. Perhaps predictably, SFBT practitioners often define this relative lack of specific skill training as another strength of the approach, as it doesn't force solution-focused school social workers to limit their interventions to specific techniques that are generated by the school social worker. For one thing, it's usually easier to get people to do things that they already know how to do (Berg, 1994; De Jong & Berg, 2002; Selekman, 2005). SFBT works hard to help clients identify the strengths and skills they already possess to address their problems, and then tries to free them up to "do more of what's working" (Berg, 1994; Newsome, 2004).

Another challenge to applying SFBT in a school involves the belief of some educators that they are there to instruct students on how to "act." Some educators who have this moral imperative may be uncomfortable with the view of SFBT of starting from where students truly are, and to work with what's there as opposed to modeling a better way to behave or think. As stated earlier, the benefit of SFBT is that it doesn't deny the presenting problems that require intervention (e.g., student defiance or work refusal). It just frames them in a way that is different from traditional school practice that typically tries to emphasize the authority of the adult over the self-determination of the student.

There is no doubt that some educators can (and do) view SFBT as excessively optimistic and too "easy" on kids. However, although SFBT does impart to clients an optimistic and future-oriented perspective, we believe that there is value in this approach. Again and again we've seen in our school practices how SFBT can elicit new ideas from clients who have traditionally viewed their problems from more fatalistic and pessimistic angles. This can involve teaching new ideas to students; so SFBT in no way has to limit the skill and authority of the teacher or school social worker using it to engage with and help a student. If anything, we have often noticed that the process of asking SFBT questions itself makes an impression on students who are unsure how to respond to treatment and are anxious about seeing a mental health professional. By starting first with a curious and hopeful stance, SFBT tries to de-escalate many potentially difficult situations and to move the focus to solving the problems that the student is having.

Finally, as a wholly client-centered treatment approach, SFBT is open to almost any intervention that is already underway in a client's life and is, in the client's view, a helpful intervention. For example, a student of ours was already taking antianxiety medication when we first met her, and part of the solution-focused treatment we conducted with her was helping her identify ways to build on the benefits she was seeing from taking her medication.

In this way, clients and school social workers can collaborate on using SFBT with other treatment models (such as CBT) that emphasize on client's setting goals and working toward them. As we discussed in Chapter 1, the portability and adaptability of SFBT in a school setting is one of the major strengths we have seen when applying this approach for the past two decades.

The Application

In Chapter 5, we will detail the several ways in which SFBT can help a school community. Here is a brief and partial list of what we've done with SFBT in our schools, which you will learn more about in Chapter 6:

1. The use of SFBT techniques to change the direction of a case study evaluation meeting to focus more on student and family strengths
2. An example of SFBT family therapy led by a school social worker in a school-based mental health clinic
3. The description of an SFBT group treatment for students struggling with anxiety
4. The story of a solution-focused needs assessment that helped a school social worker create a family health and employment fair in an impoverished community
5. The outline of an 8-week SFBT group for grandparents raising grandchildren drawing on grandparents' "old-school wisdom" for raising their grandchildren (Newsome & Kelly, 2004).

We have also included in this chapter an example of a solution-focused handout developed by Franklin and Streeter (2004) to help clients in schools set goals using SFBT techniques (see Box 2.3), and a form developed by Garner (2004) to help practitioners evaluate their school's readiness to adopt SFBT ideas (see Box 2.4).

The Research

In Chapter 3, we share more information about the effectiveness of SFBT in schools and other mental health settings. We have found in our work employing meta-analytic techniques to analyze the extant intervention

BOX 2.3 Measuring Your Success

NAME _____   DATE _____

What were your goals for the previous semester? Check the goals that were *fully* met.

When it comes to meeting your goals, what are the obstacles that get in your way?

Choose 1 of the obstacles you listed and design a plan to overcome it.

OBSTACLE	WHAT I CAN DO	RESOURCES THAT CAN HELP

Having reviewed your goals, measure your progress on a scale of 1 to 10, with 1 being no progress and 10 being goal met.

Scaling allows you to see your progress on a continuum. Consider the following criteria before marking the number that represents your progress:

- Attendance
- Number of assignments completed
- Quality of work done

Circle the number that represents your progress.

1   2   3   4   5   6   7   8   9   10

What are 3 goals that you will set for the next semester?

1.

2.

3.

Describe what it will look like, sound like, and feel like when you are meeting all of the goals you have set for yourself.

Source: Franklin, C. & Streeter, C. L. (2004) *Solution-focused accountability schools for the 21st century*. Austin: The Hogg Foundation for Mental Health, The University of Texas at Austin.

BOX 2.4 Planning Exercise for Developing Solution-Building Schools

Characteristics of a Solution-Building School

Rate your school on a scale of 1 to 10 with 1 being the characteristic is absent and 10 being the school truly represents the trait.

Faculty emphasis on building relationships with students

1	2	3	4	5	6	7	8	9	10

Attention given to individual strengths of students

1	2	3	4	5	6	7	8	9	10

Emphasis upon student choices and personal responsibility

1	2	3	4	5	6	7	8	9	10

Overall commitment to achievement and hard work

1	2	3	4	5	6	7	8	9	10

Trust in student self-evaluation

1	2	3	4	5	6	7	8	9	10

Focus on the student's future successes instead of past difficulties

1	2	3	4	5	6	7	8	9	10

Celebrating small steps toward success

1	2	3	4	5	6	7	8	9	10

Reliance on goal setting activities

1	2	3	4	5	6	7	8	9	10

Source: Creating Solution-Building Schools Training Program. Developed by Joann Garner LMSW. In C. Franklin, & C. L. Streeter (2004). *Solution-focused accountability schools for the 21st century*. Austin: The Hogg Foundation for Mental Health, The University of Texas at Austin.

studies on SFBT that this therapy has a small to moderate impact on behaviors and problems typically found in a school setting. This outcome is only slightly smaller than the typical effect of other psychotherapy treatments for some of the same behaviors and problems experienced by students (Kim, 2008).

As we note in the next chapter, in keeping with our efforts to be transparent and rigorous in this book, we can highlight the claims of SFBT's effectiveness but also caution against overstating SFBT as a technique that outperforms all other therapy approaches. In some ways, SFBT may be best viewed as an important technique to use with school clients because it facilitates conversations about client strengths while many other approaches in schools (with competing claims of effectiveness) are more rooted in medical/deficit models. What remains for further research to explore is whether strength-based approaches like SFBT produce better outcomes for students than approaches rooted in special education deficit models or social skills/psychoeducation models.

The Future

SFBT and school settings are in some ways a natural fit. School social workers are constantly struggling with large caseloads and limited time to serve all the students who need help, and the emphasis on rapid engagement and change for students can help school-based professionals meet more students and make a difference for them quickly. The goal-setting process of SFBT (involving scaling questions and asking teachers to observe behaviors that students are working on improving) can be easily adapted to the outcome-based education paperwork of Medicaid and special education to help school social workers document their effectiveness (Lever et al., 2006).

However, the challenge of finding ways to bring a solution-focused perspective using student, family, and teacher strengths into a variety of school contexts (e.g., special education staffing, disciplinary meetings, or teacher consultations) is significant and sometimes even daunting. This is particularly true as educators increasingly favor "problem-talk" about school problems using diagnostic categories derived from special education classification and psychopathology language found in the *DSM-IV* (Altshuler & Kopels, 2003; House, 2002). More research on SFBT in schools and collaboration with SFBT researchers and practitioners in schools will be essential to help make the next 25 years of solution-focused practice as fruitful and influential as the first 25 years has been.

Summary

SFBT is an approach that started in the American Midwest and has now spread all over the world, heavily influencing the last two generations of practitioners. Its main ideas, that client strengths matter, that client change is constant, and that clients can be trusted to devise solutions to their own problems, are a welcome alternative to many of the deficit-based diagnostic and treatment approaches prevalent in schools today. Solution-focused school social workers can use techniques like the miracle question, coping questions, and scaling questions to identify students' goals and strengths to help make changes in their lives.

3

■ ■ ■

SFBT and Evidence-Based Practice: The State of the Science

Introduction

Solution-focused brief therapy (SFBT) has become a popular therapeutic model for social work practice. Part of the model's appeal to social workers lies in its strengths-based focus. De Jong and Miller (1995) note that social work history is rooted in the principles of the strengths perspective, but has lacked specific tools and techniques to put strength-based practice into action. Building on Saleebey's (1992) summary of strengths-based assumptions and principles, De Jong and Miller (1995) argue that SFBT can advance social work's tradition of using strengths-based principles by providing specific intervention skills and change techniques with similar philosophical assumptions.

Practitioners from many disciplines, especially social work, have embraced SFBT because of the ease of implementing the model and its flexibility for different practice settings. In an era of accountability and evidence-based practice (EBP), however, the effectiveness of SFBT is important for social workers to consider. This chapter will discuss the importance of EBP for social work and highlight its importance for school-based practice. The chapter will also summarize the research support for SFBT and address the state of research on SFBT model when compared to other intervention models. Particular emphasis will be given to a meta-analysis study on SFBT and to a review of SFBT studies conducted in school settings.

Evidence-Based Practice

Over the last century, social workers have relied on personal experience, advice from colleagues and supervisors, relevant theory, and textbook manuals to guide their practice (Howard, McMillen, & Pollio, 2003). Current policy demands for social workers to demonstrate their effectiveness, however, are prompting social work practitioners to choose interventions that have research support (Herie & Martin, 2002). Funders and legislators, for example, expect social workers to employ best practice guidelines resulting from empirical research (Gorey, 1996). Policy makers and federal and state agencies have also pressed for evidence-based interventions that have met an acceptable threshold or number of studies that support the intervention's effectiveness with client problems. EBP originated in medicine and was transported into the mental health profession and other disciplines, including education. Medicine describes EBP as using the best available evidence to inform decisions about patient care. Physicians incorporate this evidence into their clinical experiences along with the beliefs and experiences of their patients and make decisions on what the best treatment for an individual client is. There remains much debate, however, over what constitutes "evidence" and how to decide what is "effective."

Many professions and organizations, including the education field, have attempted to adopt criteria for what constitutes an EBP (Franklin, 2006). Although standard criteria in mental health and educational practice may include standardized treatments, program evaluation, controlled trials evaluating practices, or other outcomes from scientific evaluations, it usually means an intervention is considered to have established itself if it is proved to be better than placebo or conventional treatment in two clinical trials. For example, using these criteria the evidence-based treatment would be shown, through empirical research, to have worked better in a school than the standard special education intervention that is given or no intervention.

At this time social workers do not have an agreed-upon definition or a set of criteria for EBP (Franklin & Hopson, 2007; Rubin & Parrish, 2007). The definitions of EBP discussed in social work are similar to the definitions presented in the original writings in the medical field (Sackett, Straus, Richardson, Rosenberg, & Haynes, 2000). No explicit criteria for selecting an EBP intervention have been suggested other the ones developed in the psychology field. Instead, most writings on EBP within social work emphasize on a specific process that describes how practitioners should use and appraise multiple sources of information. Gambrill (1999), for example, defines EBP as a practice that ". . . involves integrating individual practice expertise with the best available external evidence from systematic research as well as considering the values and expectations of clients" (p. 346). This definition sets the stage for establishing a collaborative and individualized process between client and social worker while making use of the best research-based information in practice decisions.

Raines (2004) uses Gambrill's process definition to stake out five steps of the EBP process for school social workers:

1. Formulating answerable questions
2. Investigating the evidence
3. Appraising the evidence
4. Applying the evidence
5. Evaluating progress

Step 1: Posing Answerable Questions in Collaboration With Clients

Following an EBP approach combines the science and art of social work practice. A collaborative approach with clients is standard in EBP where clients are informed participants. Intervention approaches are discussed with the clients, as are the rationales for the recommendations and the empirical evidence supporting the intervention options (Gambrill, 1999). Thus, research is integrated with practice when social workers are evidence based and outcomes are considered extremely important. Franklin (2007) discusses what practice might look like when social workers learn to incorporate EBPs into their daily routines. First, social workers conducting EBP continuously construct external evidence-based knowledge and compare their thoughts on cases with the advise from those external sources. This is different from routine practice because most practitioners depend on their own thinking, actions, and even "gut level" hunches for what they choose to do with their clients. Instead of relying exclusively on clinical judgments, practitioners would compare their thoughts with external sources and evaluate their options. This obviously involves critical thinking and a willingness to examine one's own assumptions and ideas.

Step 2: Investigating the Evidence

Second, social workers conducting EBP rely on external resources as extensions of their own use in their practice. From their practice training, social workers are familiar with the phrase "the use of self" with clients, but in EBP, social workers move beyond the "use of self" to learn how to use a "resourced self" (Franklin, 2007). Knowledge beyond the use of themselves might be databases like Campbell or Cochrane Collaboration (www.cochranecollaboration.org; www.campbellcollaboration.org), an online journal, a statistical decision, or a support system that provides outcome assessment and on-going feedback about one's effectiveness in practice (i.e., Lambert, Hansen, & Finch, 2001).

Steps 3 and 4: Appraising the Evidence and Applying It to Real-Life Client Problems

Third, when social workers become evidence based in their work they will use external resources as consultation tools in everyday practice and appraise evidence regularly. This will do more than merely help practitioners "stay current" with the latest evidence. Rather than view the EBP process as simply a passive one where practitioners "consume" the latest evidence, this EBP process requires practitioners to actively engage the evidence and use their critical thinking skills to apply the evidence to their actual practice context. Ideally, this process of interacting with the evidence will be shared across the social worker's practice context, with both colleagues and other clients. Because social workers routinely rely on consultation from colleagues and supervisors for their learning, the resources used must be available to everyone and become a part of supervision and consultation models.

Step 5: Evaluating Client Progress Based on Interventions Discovered During the EBP Process

Finally, social workers will evaluate the effectiveness of their practices using the evidence-based interventions and will change their approach when they are not achieving the outcomes they hoped to achieve. Social workers, for example, might use an outcome assessment tool like the Child Outcome Rating Scale, which provides a brief, 5-minute measure of outcome across four areas: individual, family, school, and an overall rating. This measure is used to assess brief interventions like SFBT and provides immediate feedback to practitioners on how the client is responding to the interventions. The Child Outcome Rating Scale has also been found to get similar results as longer measures such as The Outcome Questionnaire (OQ-45.2) and its results have been further correlated with successful outcomes in intervention (Murphy & Duncan, 2007). Springer and Franklin (2003) review other outcome assessment tools that make use of outcome information in practice.

Limitations of EBP

The EBP movement is not without its limitations. Stricker (2003) cites two concerns about the way EBPs have been defined and implemented. First, there are generalizability issues for the use of these interventions in practice settings. For example, research studies that use experimental designs, which are considered the strongest in terms of research designs, may not be effective when taken from controlled university settings to the real-world settings. Alternative explanations and causes for a specific outcome, or lack thereof, are more prevalent in real-world settings (Jensen, Hoagwood, & Trickett, 1999). Also, fully validating treatments through research is yet to be done because of the lack of finality of the evidence. At best, our evidence is in process and our knowledge is not complete. A task force from the American Psychological Association (APA), for example, attempted to develop a list of empirically validated treatments only to discover that it could not be produced. Ultimately, the task force developed a list of "empirically supported treatments" because it could not fully validate any of the treatments (Stricker, 2003). More recently, in a move that was considered by many to be a positive step forward, the APA has updated their criteria for EBP, making it more flexible by incorporating client preferences and culture into their definitions (APA Presidential Task Force on Evidence-based Practice, 2006). Given these developments and the tenuous state of research, the lists of preferred practices that currently exist have to be taken in the context of how well developed the research is at this juncture and it has to recognized that these lists subject to on-going change.

Goldman et al. (2001) cite other concerns about EBP, such as its cookie cutter approach to intervention, its unrealistic expectations of its success, and its lack of scientific information on working with certain problems. Not even in the field of medicine is there a one-size-fits-all approach to treatment because there is a tremendous amount of variability in humans and between cases (Jensen et al., 1999). This variability among clients also leads to unsuccessful cases, even when there are similar symptoms and situations. Goldman et al. (2001) continue to point out that not every problem has an EBP or solution, although this area continues to change as more research studies are added. Other important concerns identified by Goldman and Azrin (2003) include

- innovative programs that have yet to acquire an evidence base, which could lose funding;
- lack of time and support for practitioners to be trained in EBPs;

- high start-up cost for implementing EBP for administrators;
- challenges in figuring out how to finance EBPs within existing insurance and Medicaid/Medicare payment systems.

Finally, research suggests that specific models and techniques do not matter as much as common factors, such as client factors, client-practitioner relationship factors, and one's allegiance to an intervention model, suggesting that the cost of EBP interventions is not justified (Duncan, Miller, & Sparks, 2004; Lambert, 2005; Wampold, 2001).

EBP in Schools

Franklin (2006) discussed how EBPs are being transported into education and are being suggested as a standard for school mental health services and instructional areas. The Department of Education, for example, founded the *What Works Clearinghouse* (http://ies.ed.gov/ncee/wwc/) that focuses on the dissemination of EBPs in education. Criteria for EBPs in education are set by the Institute of Educational Sciences, which is the research arm of the Department of Education, in consultation with a technical services group of distinguished researchers. It is important to note that criteria for EBPs in education, like other areas of practice, are constantly being revised and that different agencies and fields of practice may not agree on the same criteria or practices. This disharmony has been discussed as a problem for practice implementation (Franklin & Hopson, 2007), as well as a genesis for improvement of the EBP approach (Duncan et al., 2004; Murphy & Duncan, 2007). Even though EBP guidelines are continuously in a process of critique and evolution, it is unlikely that mandates for research-supported practices will disappear any time soon (Herie & Martin, 2002).

With a movement toward incorporating more EBPs in schools, it becomes more important than ever for school social workers and other school-based professionals to apply the EBP process to their work. Progress in this area, however, is not without its challenges because of the limitations in empirical support for educational practices. Other more promising interventions like SFBT are too new to have completed the optimal amount of studies or may not have summarized their findings of existing studies in a way that can be recognized. This is in contrast to other popular intervention models that social workers use, such as cognitive therapy and cognitive-behavioral therapy (CBT), which have met the APA's full criteria for "well-established" treatments for various mental health issues like depression, anxiety, and panic disorders (Chambless & Ollendick, 2001).

Empirical Support for SFBT

Although there is no doubt that SFBT is popular amongst social workers in the United States and around the world, the research on its effectiveness is still limited in relation to its growing popularity (Gingerich & Eisengart, 2000; Triantafillou, 1997; Zimmerman, Prest, & Wetzel, 1997). This poses problems for both social workers who have embraced the SFBT model and the schools of social work teaching SFBT as part of their curriculum. As Gorey, Thyer, and Pawluck (1998) noted in their meta-analysis article on the effectiveness of social work practice:

> Unless more progressive systemic-structural social work models are empirically studied and the findings of such studies reported in the mainstream professional press, it is likely that future funding opportunities for them and thus for their great potential for preventive and therapeutic benefits will be lost to future clients. (p. 273)

Fortunately, past research studies have shown that SFBT is promising as an effective intervention, and research on this model continues to grow by the year.

Early Research Studies on SFBT

Two of the earliest studies on the effectiveness of SFBT were conducted by the team at the Brief Family Therapy Center (BFTC). De Jong and Hopwood (1996) provide an overview of the first study conducted by Kiser (1988), which consisted of follow-up surveys (6, 12, and 18 months after termination of therapy) of clients to determine whether they had met their goals or felt they had made significant progress. Results showed 80% success rate, with 65.6% meeting their goals and 14.7% making significant improvements. At the 18-month follow-up, 86% of the clients contacted reported success. This study, however, used subjective measures and did not use a control group or comparison group, which threatens internal and external validity. Furthermore, the researchers in this study counted a client's report of "some progress" as success but did not use other measures to confirm the outcomes (Stalker, Levene, & Coady, 1999).

The second study, conducted by De Jong and Hopwood (1996), involved 275 clients seen at BFTC from November 1992 to August 1993. Similar to Kiser's (1988) study, participants were contacted 7 to 9 months after termination of therapy and asked whether they had met their goals. In addition, therapists asked each participant scaling questions (1 being "problem is worse than before" and 10 being "problem solved") at each session to gauge progress. The final scaling question score was then subtracted from the first scaling question score to come up with an intermediate outcome measurement. These scores were then categorized into three groups: score −3 to 0 equals "no progress," score 1 to 3 equals "moderate progress," and score 4 to 8 equals "significant progress."

Results from this study indicated that out of 136 participant responses, 45% reported meeting their goals, 32% reported some progress towards their goal, and 23% reporting no progress after termination of therapy. On the intermediate score measure, 141 responses were calculated on the basis of the therapists' session notes. Results from this measure showed that 25% reported significant progress, 49% reported moderate progress, and 26% reported no progress. Limitations of this study are similar to the first study because it lacked multiple, standardized measures. Despite the lack of rigorous designs in these two early studies, the initial success and positive results were impressive enough to warrant further research on this promising model.

Results From a Review of Research on SFBT

Gingerich and Eisengart (2000) conducted the first systematic qualitative review of all the controlled 15 outcome studies on SFBT up to 1999. All of these studies used either a comparison group or single-case repeated measures design to measure various client behaviors or functioning. The studies were divided into three groups according to the degree of experimental control employed (see Tables 3.1–3.3). Five studies met the well-controlled standard, four studies met the moderately controlled standard, and six studies met the poorly controlled standard.

They defined a well-controlled study as having met at least five of the following criteria:

1. Compared the experiential group with a control group
2. Used random assignments for treatment and control groups or an acceptable single-case design
3. Used a large sample
4. Focused on a well-defined disorder
5. Had outcome measure that showed validity and reliability, and
6. Used treatment manuals

Table 3.1 Gingerich and Eisengart (2000) Well-Controlled Studies

AUTHOR	POPULATION	SAMPLE SIZE	SETTING	SESSIONS	DESIGN TYPE
Sundstrom (1993)	College students (All females)	40	University	1	Pretest–posttest with control group
Zimmerman, Jacobsen, MacIntyre, and Watson (1996)	Parents	42	Marriage and family therapy clinic	6	Pretest–posttest with control group
Cockburn et al. (1997)	Orthopedic patients	48	Rehabilitation program	6	Solomon four group
Lindforss and Magnusson (1997)	Adult criminals	60	Swedish prison	5	Pretest–posttest with control group
Seagram (1997)	Youth offenders	40	Secure youth facility	10	Pretest–posttest with control group

Table 3.2 Gingerich and Eisengart (2000) Moderately Controlled Studies

AUTHOR	POPULATION	SAMPLE SIZE	SETTING	SESSIONS	DESIGN TYPE
Littrell, Malia, and Vanderwood (.995)	9–12 graders	61	High school	3	Posttest only with comparison group
LaFountain and Garner (1996)	Elementary and high school students	311	Elementary and high school	8	Pretest–posttest with comparison group
Triantafillou (1997)	Children	12	Children's residential treatment agency	4	Posttest only with comparison group
Zimmerman et al. (1997)	Couples	36	Marriage and family therapy clinic	6	Pretest–posttest with comparison group

Table 3.3 Gingerich and Eisengart (2000) Poorly Controlled Studies

AUTHOR	POPULATION	SAMPLE SIZE	SETTING	SESSIONS	DESIGN TYPE
Polk (1996)	Adults	1	Employee assistance program	6	Single subject AB
Eakes Walsh, Markowksi, Cain, and Swanson (1997)	Families	10	Mental health clinic	5	Pretest–posttest comparison group
Franklin (1997)	Adolescents	3	Youth runaway and homeless shelter	5	Single subject AB
Geil (1998)	Elementary school children and teachers	8 student–teacher pairs	Elementary school	12	Single subject AB
Lambert et al. (1998)	Adult couples	72	Private practice	2–7	Pretest–posttest with comparison group
Sundman (1997)	Adults	382	Public social service agencies	Not reported	Posttest only with comparison group

Moderately controlled studies met four of the previously mentioned criteria, and poorly controlled studies met three or fewer of the criteria.

The five well-controlled studies reported significant benefits from SFBT, with four out of these five reporting statistically significant better results than those no treatment or institutional services. All these studies had a sample size of at least 40 participants, with the number of sessions ranging from 1 to 10. The types of participants and settings were diverse, ranging from college students at a university to adult criminals at a Swedish prison. None of these five well-controlled studies, however, met all of the stringent criteria suggested in the preceding text. All five studies also used different populations, which is a problem for showing that the results repeat themselves through replication. Because of these reasons, the authors could not conclude that SFBT has been shown to be efficacious. They suggested, on then basis of these findings, that these five studies provide initial support for the effectiveness of SFBT.

All the four moderately controlled studies used comparison groups of similar people in their research design stage, but only half gathered posttest scores, which means that they did not use a very rigorous research design. The number of sessions per study was brief, ranging from three to eight sessions, and sample sizes varied from 12 to 311. The types of participants and settings were not as diverse as the well-controlled studies, with three out of the four studies involving adolescents at their schools or residential treatment agency. The other study was conducted at a marriage and family therapy clinic with adult couples. All four of these moderately controlled studies reported statistically significant results favoring SFBT.

Finally, six studies were deemed poorly controlled by Gingerich and Eisengart (2000) because they employed three or fewer of the criteria identified in the preceding text. Half of the studies employed a single-subject AB research design, which is helpful for practice evaluation but not a strong enough research design to discover if an intervention works. The other three used a comparison group but left out other important elements on the aforementioned criteria, such as not randomly assigning participants or using a thorough description of the problem area being addressed or intervention being used (i.e., treatment manual). The number of sessions per study ranged from 2 to 12, with one study not reporting the number of sessions. Sample sizes ranged from 1 to 382 and participants for four of the six studies were adults while those for the other two were adolescents. The settings were varied, ranging from mental health clinics to homeless shelters. Like the five well-controlled studies, these six poorly controlled studies had a similar general conclusion about the effectiveness of SFBT. Because of the limitations of the methods for conducting research on SFBT in these six studies, however, it is difficult to draw firm conclusions on the effectiveness of SFBT.

SFBT Meta-analysis Study

The good news is that since Gingerich and Eisengart's (2000) review, there has been a rise in the number of research studies conducted examining the effectiveness of SFBT. To advance the research on SFBT and to provide an updated review for practitioners, a meta-analysis was conducted by Kim (2008). Meta-analysis is a quantitative review method that allows researchers to combine and synthesize existing studies and reanalyze them in order to determine overall outcomes. The effect size statistics is used to report the outcomes of the review. By calculating effect sizes, the meta-analyst converts measures in primary studies into a common metric of treatment effect or relation between variables. It is possible to achieve small, medium, or large effect sizes when calculating the outcomes. Most practice researchers prefer to see medium or large effects when they are evaluating the overall effectiveness of an intervention. It is unusual, however, to achieve more than a small effect size when analyzing more rigorous studies or when evaluating studies conducted in community-based settings. See Box 3.1 for a formal definition and description of meta-analysis.

Kim (2008) synthesized SFBT outcome studies to determine its overall effectiveness and thus provided more empirical information on its effectiveness. Because these studies vary in regards to research designs, populations, and findings, a research synthesis using meta-analytic procedures appears to be a good approach to examine the state of the empirical evidence for SFBT.

The main research question for Kim's (2008) meta-analysis study was how effective is SFBT for externalizing behavior problems (e.g., aggression and conduct problems), internalizing behavior problems (e.g., depression and self-esteem), and family or relationship problems. These were the most frequent outcomes measured in the studies on SFBT and are of considerable interest to social workers. The results from the literature search on SFBT studies produced 22 studies that met the criteria to be included in the meta-analysis. The 22 studies included in the meta-analysis were divided and grouped into three categories on the basis of the outcome problem

BOX 3.1 Description of Meta-analysis

A meta-analysis integrates findings from a collection of individual studies with similar construct to determine the magnitude of the treatment effect (Glass, 1976). Instead of relying on anecdotal evidence, meta-analytic procedures can be used to synthesize quantitative results from studies to calculate effect sizes, which measure the strength and direction of a relationship. The larger the magnitude of the effect size, the stronger the treatment effect. Confidence intervals can also be calculated to measure the precision of the effect size estimate. Furthermore, if there is heterogeneity in effect sizes across studies, then predictor variables can be examined to help explain this variability (Hall, Tickle-Degnen, Rosenthal, & Mosteller, 1994). The statistical method of meta-analysis has been used to identify effective practice methods developed and evaluated by social workers since the 1980s (Reid, 2002). A solution-focused brief therapy meta-analysis can add to the progress by providing a comprehensive effort to systematically evaluate its effectiveness through the aggregation of multiple outcome studies (Corcoran, Miller, & Bultman, 1997).

each study targeted (i.e., externalizing behavior problems, internalizing behavior problems, and family and relationship problems). Each of the three categories had between 8 and 12 studies, each with 5 studies (Huang, 2001; Marinaccio, 2001; Franklin, Moore, & Hopson (2008); Seagram, 1997; Triantafillou, 2002) being included in more than one category because they examined more than one outcome problem (see Tables 3.4–3.6).

Kim's (2008) meta-analysis review found that SFBT demonstrated small, but positive, treatment effects favoring the SFBT group on the outcome measures. The overall weighted mean effect size estimates were .13 for externalizing behavior problems, .26 for internalizing problem behaviors, and .26 for family and relationship problems. Only the magnitude of the effect for internalizing behavior problems was statistically significant at the $p < .05$ level, thereby indicating that the treatment outcome for the SFBT group is different from the treatment outcome for the control group.

The small effect sizes calculated in Kim's SFBT meta-analysis are only slightly smaller than other effect sizes calculated in similar social science research. As Table 3.7 highlights, SFBT effect sizes are comparable to those in other psychotherapy and social work meta-analysis studies when conducted under real-world conditions.

The meta-analysis for SFBT did not achieve the medium and large effect sizes that researchers like to see in outcomes. As noted, however, it is unusual to achieve anything above small effect sizes when evaluating applied research studies in community settings and this would be the case with SFBT research. To illustrate, the small effect sizes calculated in this SFBT meta-analysis are only slightly smaller than the effect sizes calculated for psychotherapy. For example, psychotherapy's mean overall effect size on adolescent depression, when including dissertations and using more rigorous effect size calculations than previous meta-analyses on this subject, was moderate (.34) with a range of −.66 to 2.02. In addition, studies on the effectiveness of psychotherapy on adolescent depression that were conducted in real-world settings had a small overall weighted mean effect size of .24 (Weisz, McCarty, & Valeri, 2006). Similarly, Babcock, Green, and Robie (2004) cite other meta-analytic studies on psychotherapy with small effect size results due to difficulties in treating externalizing problem behaviors like aggression (Loesel & Koeferl, 1987; Weisz, Weiss, Han, Granger, & Morton, 1995). Therefore, while the results from Kim's (2008) study found small treatment effects for SFBT, other meta-analyses on psychotherapy found only slightly better or equal results, depending on the research study setting.

Current Research in School Settings

While the preceding section focuses primarily on all SFBT research, several recent studies have focused on SFBT work in school settings. The application of SFBT with students and in school settings has grown over the past 10 years and continues to be an area of interest for researchers, school social workers, and other school-based professionals. SFBT has been applied in school settings to a number of problems, including student behavioral and emotional issues, academic problems, and social skills. Table 3.8 summarizes some of the more rigorous experimental and quasi-experimental design studies on SFBT in schools published in peer-reviewed journals.

As Table 3.8 highlights, five quasi-experimental design studies and one single-case design study on SFBT in schools were published since 2000, with most studies being published within the past 2 years. The results from most

Table 3.4 Externalizing Behavior Outcome Results

AUTHOR	POPULATION	SAMPLE SIZE	SESSION NUMBER	OUTCOME MEASURE	EFFECT SIZE (d)	CI
Franklin et al. (2007)	Students	85	N/A	Credits earned	.47	(.03, .91)
Gallardo-Cooper (1997)	Mothers and teachers	66	1	Eyberg Child Behavior Scale, Sutter-Eyberg Student Behavior Scale	−.14	(−.56, .28)
Huang (2001)	Couples	39	8	Conflict Tactics Scale, Scaling Questions	−.43	(−1.24, .38)
Ingersoll-Dayton et al. (1999)	Elderly	21	7	Modified Caretaker Obstreperous-Behavior Rating Assessment	.32	(−.30, .94)
Marinaccio (2001)	Students, mothers, and teachers	120	4.5	Behavioral Assessment System for Children— conduct and aggression subscale	−.25	(−.56, .06)

Study	Population	n		Measures		CI
Franklin et al. (2008)	Students	59	5.8	Achenbach Behavioral Checklist—teacher and student externalizing behavior subscale	.74	(.20, 1.28)
Newsome (2004)	Students	52	8	Grades and Attendance	0	(−.55, .55)
Seagram (1997)	Youth offenders	40	10	Jesness Behavior Checklist, Carlson Psychological Survey, solution-focused questions, Test of Self-Conscious Affect	.17	(−.47, .81)
Triantafillou (2002)	Children	30	4	Devereux Scales of Mental Disorder—externalizing score and critical pathology score, Social Skills Rating System, total number of problem behaviors, total number of physical restraints	.17	(−.59, .93)

Table 3.5 Internalizing Behavior Outcome Results

AUTHOR	POPULATION	SAMPLE SIZE	SESSION NUMBER	OUTCOME MEASURE	EFFECT SIZE (d)	CI
Bozeman (1999)	Psychiatric patients	52	3	Beck Depression Inventory, Nowotny Hope Scale	.56	(−.01, 1.13)
Cook (1998)	Students	68	6	Piers-Harris Children's Self-Concept Scale	.28	(−.21, .77)
Huang (2001)	Couples	39	8	Beck Depression Inventory	.23	(−.58, 1.04)
Leggett (2004)	Students	67	11	Coopersmith Self-Esteem Inventory, Children's Hope Scale	.04	(−.45, .53)
Marinaccio (2001)	Students	48	4.5	Student Report of Personality, Behavior Assessment System for Children— adaptability, anxiety, social skills subscales	.06	(−.24, .37)

Franklin et al. (2008)	Students	59	5.8	Achenbach Behavioral Checklist—Teacher & Student internalizing behavior subscale	.74	(.20, 1.28)
Seagram (1997)	Youth offenders	40	10	Coopersmith Self-Esteem Inventory	−.06	(−.70, .58)
Springer et al. (2000)	Students	10	6	Hare Self-Esteem Scale	.57	(−.91, 2.05)
Sundstrom (1993)	College students	40	1	Beck Depression Inventory, Depression Adjective Checklist	1.18	(.48, 1.88)
Triantafillou (2002)	Children	30	4	Devereux Scales of Mental Disorder-internalizing score	−.46	(−1.23, .31)
Villalba (2002)	Students	59	6	Piers-Harris Children's Self-Concept Scale	.11	(−.41, .63)
Wettersten (2002)	Adults	65	25	Brief Symptom Inventory	.26	(−.24, .76)

Table 3.6 Family and Relationship Outcome Results

AUTHOR	POPULATION	SAMPLE SIZE	SESSION NUMBER	OUTCOME MEASURE	EFFECT SIZE (d)	CI
Adams et al. (1991)	Families	40	9.5	Immediate Outcome Rating Scale—Goal Clarity, Optimism, and Compliance	.70	(.04, 1.36)
Cockburn et al. (1997)	Orthopedic patients	48	6	Family Crisis Oriented Personal Evaluation Scales, Psychological Adjustment to Illness Scale—Self Report	1.23	(.30, 2.16)
Eakes et al. (1997)	Families	10	5	Family Environment Scale	.52	(−.38, 1.42)
Huang (2001)	Couples	39	8	Marital Status Inventory, Dyadic Adjustment Scale	.25	(−.56, 1.06)
Sundman (1997)	Adults	200	N/A	Therapist and client completed questionnaire	0	(−.28, .28)
Triantafillou (2002)	Children	30	4	Parent–Adolescent Communication Scale, Family Adaptability and Cohesion Scales II	−.56	(−1.33, .21)
Zimmerman et al. (1996)	Parents	42	6	Parent Skills Inventory	.17	(−.52, .86)
Zimmerman et al. (1997)	Couples	36	6	Dyadic Adjustment Scale	.29	(−.20, .78)

Table 3.7 Comparison of Meta-analyses

AUTHOR	TREATMENT INTERVENTION	POPULATION	OUTCOME MEASURE	EFFECT SIZE
Kim (2008)	Solution-focused brief therapy	Various	Externalizing problems	.13
			Internalizing problems	.26
			Family and relationship problems	.26
Weisz et al. (2006)	Psychotherapy (overall)	Adolescents	Depression	.34
	Psychotherapy under real-world clinical setting	Adolescents	Depression	.24
Babcock et al. (2004)	Domestic violence treatments	Domestically violent males	Police reports	.18
			Partner reports	.18
Gorey (1996)	General social work practice	Various	Various	.36

Table 3.8 SFBT Studies in Schools

STUDY	DESIGN	OUTCOME MEASURE	SAMPLE SIZE	SAMPLE POPULATION	RESULTS
Corcoran (2006)	Quasi-experimental	Conners' Parent Rating Scale Feelings, Attitudes, and Behaviors Scale for Children	86	Students aged 5–17	No significant differences between groups with both improving at posttest. This lack of difference may be because the comparison group received treatment as usual, which had many cognitive-behavior therapy components that had been empirically validated.
Franklin Biever, Moore, Clemons, and Scamardo (2001)	Single case	Conners' Teacher Rating Scale	7	Middle school students 10–12 years old	Five of seven (71%) improved per teachers report.
Franklin et al. (2007)	Quasi-experimental	Grades Attendance		At-risk high school students	SFBT sample had statistically significant higher average proportion of credits earned to credits attempted than the comparison sample. Both groups decreased in the attendance mean per semester; however, the comparison group

					showed a higher proportion of school days attended to school days for the semester. Authors suggested that the attendance between groups may not be a fair comparison because SFBT group worked on a self-paced curriculum and could decrease their attendance when completed.
Franklin et al. (2008)	Quasi-experimental	Child Behavior Checklist (CBCL)—Youth Self-Report Form—internalizing and CBCL externalizing Teacher's Report Form—internalizing and externalizing score	67	Middle school students	Internalizing & Externalizing score for the Teacher Report Form showed SFBT group declined below clinical level by posttest and remained there at follow-up while comparison group changed little. Internalizing score for the Youth Self Report Form showed no difference between the groups. Externalizing score showed SFBT group dropped below the clinical level and continued to drop at follow-up.

(continued)

Table 3.8 Continued

STUDY	DESIGN	OUTCOME MEASURE	SAMPLE SIZE	SAMPLE POPULATION	RESULTS
Newsome (2004)	Quasi-experimental	Grades Attendance	52	Middle school students	SFBT group increased from a mean score of 1.58 to a mean score of 1.69 while grades for the comparison group decreased from a mean score of 1.66 to a score of 1.48. No difference on attendance measure.
Springer et al. (2000)	Quasi-experimental	Hare Self-Esteem Scale	10	Hispanic elementary students	SFBT group make significant improvements on the Hare Self-Esteem Scale, whereas the comparison group's scores remained the same. However, no significant differences were found between the SFBT and comparison groups at the end of the study on the self-esteem scale.

of the studies were mixed, thereby limiting the ability to draw definitive conclusions. Initial impressions of these results may be misleading, however, as the authors of the studies note several factors that may have influenced the mixed results. For example, Corcoran's (2006) study found no difference between groups at posttest, but this may be due to the fact that SFBT was being compared to a comparison group that received a CBT–based intervention, where the techniques have been empirically validated. One could look at this as SFBT not being any better, but not any worse than the treatment students usually receive, which is based on CBT.

Studies by Franklin et al. (2007) and Newsome (2004) cite curriculum program and sample issues as important factors in their null results on attendance outcome measures. In the study by two of the authors of the book, Franklin et al. (2007), the relationship between attendance and academic performance appears to be minimized. The SFBT students attended a school (Garza School in Austin, Texas) where a self-paced content mastery curriculum permitted students to move at their own pace. This meant that students could complete requirements faster or slower than they would in a regular school (the comparison school in this study). If a student mastered the content of a course quickly, then he or she could finish the course requirement before the end of the semester and not go to class thereafter. However, the school district still counted the student as being absent for each day he or she didn't attend, regardless of the fact that the student finished the course content. Therefore, the relationship between attendance and performance was mitigated by the nature of the curriculum and self-paced learning style (see Chapter 5 for more details). Future studies of SFBT's impact on attendance would need to deal with this variable in assessing how SFBT might positively impact students with attendance problems.

Newsome's (2004) article also found no difference between groups on attendance but cite sample issues as a possible explanation. The author states that while the students in the SFBT group had attendance problems during the previous school year, these same students were actually attending school regularly during the following academic year in which the study took place. Therefore school absences were not a problem with the SFBT sample at any point during the research study like they were in the previous year when they were selected to participate in the experiment but hadn't received the intervention yet. The lack of difference in absences between the SFBT and comparison group is not surprising because both groups were attending regularly during the research study period.

Finally, Springer, Lynch, and Rubin (2000) found no differences between the SFBT group and comparison group on the Hare Self-Esteem Scale at the end of a 6-week student support group, thereby not finding any support for the effectiveness of SFBT in raising self-esteem. One main concern, however, about the generalizability of the study is the use of self-esteem as a dependent variable. Many researchers attempt providing interventions that try to improve adolescents' self-esteem with the hope that this will lead to better school performance and behavior. However, since the publication of the Springer et al. (2000) study, questions about the validity of using self-esteem as a measure of behavioral and academic improvements have been raised. Baumeister, Campbell, Krueger, and Vohs (2003) recently examined the literature on the concept of self-esteem and found that high self-esteem does not lead to good school performance and may actually increase risky behaviors in adolescents such as smoking, drug use, and engaging in sex at an early age. They found little to no support for boosting self-esteem in an effort to improve academic and behavioral outcomes in adolescents. Hence, the use of SFBT to help increase self-esteem may not be appropriate if the ultimate goal is to reduce risky behaviors and increase academic success.

These types of mixed results are not unusual for studies conducted in real-world practice settings (viz., effectiveness study), which are more common in social work research, as opposed to research studies conducted in clinical settings (viz., efficacy studies), which are more common in psychology. Efficacy studies conducted in clinical settings are able to control for many factors, such as intervention training, treatment fidelity, and client selection that effectiveness studies conducted in practical settings are not able to control for in their studies (Connor-Smith & Weisz, 2003). A major problem with efficacy studies, however, is the diminished results found when models are transferred from the clinical setting to real-world settings, such as schools (Southam-Gerow, Weisz, & Kendall, 2003; Weisz, 2004). In contrast, all of the studies in Table 3.7 are conducted under real-world settings and therefore show promise under typical clinical practice situations, unlike the optimal clinical efficacy studies that have shown to be ineffective when the model is transferred into clinical practice settings (Kim, 2008).

An important feature in these recent studies is the positive results found in almost all of the studies for those students receiving SFBT. Although there may not be enough studies to draw definitive conclusions about the effectiveness of SFBT, the use of rigorous research designs in real world settings with increased sample sizes and statistical power does provide support for it to be looked upon as a promising therapy model. In fact, all the studies described in Table 3.8 use either an experimental or quasi-experimental design, which helps reduce threats to internal validity (Rubin & Babbie, 2005). The more recent outcome studies on SFBT have moved beyond follow-up survey studies of the past and have begun to employ more rigorous well-controlled study designs, thereby lending more credibility to interpretations of the results obtained. In fact, viewed practically, SFBT is offered with few clinical sessions and has shown to perform in a manner similar to other therapy conditions conducted in community settings with longer therapy sessions.

Research Implications for Practice in Schools

Given the state of the research on SFBT, social work practitioners may be wondering, "Is SFBT effective?" and if so, "With what client populations does SFBT work?" The state of the research on SFBT and the limited numbers of studies available only provides tentative answers to these practice questions at this point. Therefore, the answer to these questions is a qualified yes and no. The one overall area where SFBT appears to be effective is with internalizing behavior problems such as depression, anxiety, and self-concept. SFBT doesn't appear to be as effective with externalizing behavior problem such as hyperactivity, conduct problems, and aggression or with family and relationship problems, though each of these two areas do have studies showing small effect sizes (Adams, Piercy, & Jurich, 1991; Cockburn, Thomas, & Cockburn, 1997; Franklin et al., 2007; Franklin et al., 2008). Again, it should be noted that while the effect size estimates were small for all three outcome areas, they were no different or slightly lower than other well-researched psychotherapy interventions.

SFBT may be beneficial for those difficult clients who have been unsuccessful in resolving problems. For example, Franklin et al. (2008) conducted a study with children in a school setting who were having classroom and behavioral problems that could not be resolved by teachers and principals. They conducted individual sessions of SFBT combined with teacher consultations. After receiving the SFBT intervention, teachers reported on a standardized measure (The Connors Teacher Rating Scale) that the children's behavior problems significantly improved. Children also rated themselves and reported that their behavior had improved. The effect sizes were medium to large for the changes achieved.

Another advantage of SFBT for social work practice is that this model can be effective in helping to create change in the target problem quickly and identify specific goals collaborated by both the client and social worker. Across the three different outcome categories reported in the meta-analysis, several individual studies found large effect sizes with six or fewer therapy sessions (Cockburn et al., 1997; Franklin et al., 2008; Sundstrom, 1993). Furthermore, many of the studies examining the effectiveness of SFBT included in the meta-analysis are conducted in real-world settings and therefore show promise under typical practice situations unlike the optimal clinical efficacy studies that have shown to be ineffective when the model is transferred into clinical practice settings.

Although this chapter focused on examining the state of research on SFBT and its effectiveness, it is important to keep in mind that common factors play an important role in treatment effectiveness. Common factors are less about specific techniques and are more about the therapeutic relationships and individual characteristics that help bring about change in clients. These common factors focus more on the personality and behavior of social workers, expectations of change, and engagement in therapy-relevant activities (Kazdin, 2005). Trying to determine whether SFBT is more effective than other therapy models may prove futile because studies have shown that all therapies are basically equal in effectiveness, and other nontreatment factors common across therapy models may bring about therapeutic change independent of the social worker's specific techniques (Lambert, 2005; Reisner, 2005; Wampold, 2001). What is more essential in research is for SFBT to demonstrate superiority to some control condition that was on a waiting list for services or received no treatment (Chambless, 2002; Duncan et al., 2004).

Future Areas for Research

Despite the promising results, outcomes from the SFBT meta-analysis should be looked upon with some caution because of the limited number of studies available for inclusion in the meta-analysis. The relatively small number of studies included in the meta-analysis not only reduces statistical power but also limits generalizability. In other words, we are not sure whether the statistics we are using can detect the outcomes and we cannot say for sure that the findings will apply to other settings. One possible explanation for the relatively small effect size estimates in the meta-analysis, for example, may be a result of measurement error. The types of measures used, especially for internalizing behavior problems, may be inappropriate for detecting clinical changes. Almost half the studies examining internalizing behavior problems used self-esteem or self-concept measures with adolescents in school settings with the belief that higher self-esteem will result in positive outcomes. Although self-esteem does have a high correlation with happiness, improving self-esteem through therapeutic interventions does not produce better academic performance or outcomes (Baumeister et al., 2003).

Concerns also arise about the evaluation of treatment fidelity by the therapists conducting the SFBT sessions and their training level in the model. Treatment fidelity requires us to answer very important questions. Do these practitioners know how to do SFBT and how well did they do it in the sessions? Results on the effectiveness of SFBT could be misleading if practitioners weren't adequately trained or did not adhere to the core components of the therapy model. One possible approach to improving treatment fidelity in outcome research studies is to utilize a treatment manual to further improve adherence to the SFBT model. However, using a treatment manual has not been demonstrated to improve practice to a great extent in the real world (Duncan et al., 2004). Most therapy models that are deemed evidence based, however, are manualized practices that allow for some consistency amongst researchers conducting the studies. Currently, the Solution-Focused Brief Therapy Association in North America and the European Brief Therapy Association in Europe have created treatment manuals that will aid in improving intervention fidelity. Preparation of SFBT treatment manuals is still in progress, but the introduction of these manuals demonstrates that SFBT adherents are getting serious about training and fidelity on the model. Excerpts from the treatment manual developed by the Solution-Focused Brief Therapy Association are contained in Box 3.2. Improving treatment fidelity in future studies and making sure that clinicians conducting SFBT sessions have extensive training in the SFBT model will help ensure confidence in the results obtained from the primary study.

To confidently determine the effectiveness of SFBT through a meta-analytic review, more primary studies with larger sample sizes and rigorous research designs are needed. In addition, studies using experimental designs need to utilize standardized measures that are sensitive enough to measure brief intervention changes and that possess satisfactory clinical sensitivity, especially for internalizing behavior problems. To help reduce the number of studies excluded from meta-analysis, studies should publish enough statistical information to calculate effect sizes, such as means and standard

Therapist Characteristics and Requirements

SFBT should posses the requisite training and certification in mental health discipline, the requisite training and certification in chemical dependency treatment, and specialized training in SFBT. The ideal SFBT would posses: 1) a minimum of a Master's degree in a counseling discipline, such as counseling, social work, marriage and family therapy, psychology, or psychiatry; 2) a license or certificate in a clinical area; 3) formal training and supervision in solution-focused therapy, either via a university class or a series of workshops and training. Therapists who seem to embrace and excel as solution focused therapists have these characteristics: 1) Are warm and friendly; 2) Are naturally positive and supportive (often are told they "see the good in people"); 3) Are open minded and flexible to new ideas; 4) Are excellent listeners, especially the ability to listen for clients' previous solutions embedded in "problem-talk"; 5) Are tenacious and patient. (Excerpts from the Solution-Focused Therapy Treatment Manual for Working with Individuals Research Committee of the Solution-Focused Brief Therapy Association, 2006, p. 13).

deviations scores for both pretest and posttest groups and experimental and control groups.

Summary

This chapter discussed the importance of EBP. Definitions of and criteria for effectiveness may vary somewhat across disciplines but school social workers should make every effort to incorporate the five-stage EBP process model in order to locate and apply the best available evidence to serve their students. EBP also has limitations and this chapter reviewed several challenges this approach must overcome if it is to be successfully implemented in schools and other applied settings.

The chapter also summarized the research support for SFBT and addressed the state of research on SFBT model as compared to other intervention models. Particular emphasis was given to reviewing a meta-analysis study on SFBT conducted by Kim (2008), as well as a review of SFBT studies conducted in school settings. The research on SFBT is limited at this point in its development but the studies that exist consistently demonstrate that SFBT is a promising approach that deserves further research with better research designs. Two areas where SFBT shows the most promise are in its ability to handle difficult problems that have not responded to other interventions and the brevity with which results can be achieved.

4

WOWW: Coaching Teachers to See the Solutions in Their Classrooms

Educational research on student behavior and classroom achievement increasingly shows that creative, engaged teachers are able to manage classrooms more effectively than burnt-out teachers or teachers who feel overwhelming pressure to teach to tests (Evertson et al., 2006; Responsive Classroom, 2006). Likewise, teachers who are able to demonstrate consistent and effective classroom management tend to report having the following strengths and supports in their personal life and school environment (O'Hanlon & Clifton, 2004). The WOWW program ("Working on What Works") strives to empower teachers in regular and special education settings to recognize their own strength as well as those of their students in setting goals and developing a shared focus as learners. It was first developed by solution-focused brief therapy (SFBT) pioneers Insoo Kim Berg and Lee Shilts, in Florida in 2002 (Berg & Shilts, 2005). After being piloted in urban schools in Fort Lauderdale, Florida, the program has been implemented in other cities, including in several schools we have worked with in Chicago (Berg & Shilts, 2004; Kelly & Bluestone-Miller, 2007). In this chapter, we will share some of our own preliminary findings on WOWW's success in helping students and teachers as well as other pilot data on WOWW we've been able to find.

Looking for Solutions in the Teachers' Lounge

I got my pasta out of the microwave and sat down with some teacher colleagues one day before a holiday break. Before I could take my first bite, one teacher colleague grilled me about what I thought about her class. "You work with half of them in your office, aren't they wild?" asked Betty. "Jeannie (her 2nd-grade teacher colleague) told me that these 3rd graders were going to be hell on wheels for me, and she was right! And the worst two are Sal and Carlos; oh, why did I have to get those two?" Outwardly, I was speechless, as I could tell Betty was just getting started. Inside, I was thinking that it might be time for me to offer more to Betty and her class than just pulling out the kids in her class who had social work services on their individualized education plans (IEPs).

Soon, other teachers at the table joined in with their stories of Sal and Carlos, one sharing that she works on lunch duty on Fridays and thinks that Sal "shouldn't be out at lunch until he can get himself together." Another told a story about how Carlos' dad dropped him off at school, and she heard from another mom that she smelled alcohol on his breath. "There you go, that's what I have to deal with," Betty said, and turned back to me. "So what do you think?"

I took a deep breath, agreed with her that the kids in her class were tough, and told her that I was interested in trying this new program in her class. It was called "WOWW" and I thought it might be a good way for me to help get her class under control. She said she'd think about it, but quickly added, "but you make sure that the principal knows that she better be ready for me to start sending Sal and Carlos down to her if things don't change soon!"

One of the toughest places to sit as a school social worker can be the teachers' lounge. The negative energy in there can be thick, as good-natured venting and laughing about job stress can give way to colleagues turning to you and asking questions about the kids you work with ("what's *wrong* with Billy, anyway?") or offering not-so-professional takes on what makes it hard for some kids at school ("those Smith boys are all the same; I taught their dad too and he was just as crazy"). Being in these situations pushes lots of our professional and ethical buttons, as we struggle to figure out how to respond (and finish our lunch as well). Although we're still not fans of kicking back in the lounge and gossiping about kids, we have, through SFBT coaching interventions like WOWW, learned to see our teacher colleagues more sympathetically, as they struggle to grapple with the many demands on their time, and the complicated nature of the kids that come through their door each day.

Teachers Are People, Too

It is tempting and even easy to see the story of the teacher's lounge as evidence that teachers are perhaps as crazy as the kids they call crazy.

It is also tempting to view the role of the school social worker as one where you work with the primary client in most referral situations— the student—in an environment that you largely control, that is, your own office, and leave the behavioral acting-out and general craziness that takes place in the classroom for teachers, principals, and disciplinarians to handle. After all, for most of us in schools, we are in no obvious position to supervise, discipline, or correct behaviors that are exhibited in classrooms. While it's clear that most of us wouldn't want the dual role of disciplining the very students we're also trying to counsel, what about our feelings toward our teaching colleagues? How many of us have had "those" classrooms, where we know that kids are likely to be yelled at and have their particular social/emotional needs ignored or minimized? Wouldn't it be at least momentarily satisfying if we could just "stop" the restrictive behavior of the teachers and see whether the kids responded any differently?

Teachers aren't monsters, not any more than the kids are. Teachers enter schools excited to give their students a love for learning and to be a person they can look up to. Again and again, teachers fresh to the field report a "love of children" and "a passion for teaching" as part of their reasons for choosing the teaching profession (Roehrig, Presley, & Talotta, 2002). Yet, research also shows that 50% of those same excited, idealistic teachers will leave the profession of teaching altogether after 5 years (National Education Association, 2006). This is evidence that something is happening in those initial years to bring so many teachers to the same conclusion that teaching isn't for them. What can we learn from the research on teacher retention and burnout?

First and foremost, we would do well to think of all our teacher colleagues in the same way we might think of our clients: they are complicated and interesting individuals who bring a multitude of strengths and challenges to their work. In short, they're human and if anything, by doing an SFBT-based intervention like WOWW with them, we help more of that humanity in their teaching practice to emerge, while also giving them the chance to share the stresses of the classroom in appropriate and solution-focused ways with the WOWW coach and the teacher's students.

Just as we are largely not occupying disciplinary roles in schools, we are usually not involved in supervising and evaluating teacher performance (Constable, 2006). This could be viewed either as a burden (having to put up with teachers and a school environment that can at times seem hostile to kids), or can present its own SFBT opportunity. We offer the WOWW program as one way to help multiple levels of the school contextual system: helping teachers see their own strengths, helping students work together more effectively as a group, and helping both teachers and students learn how to be more respectful and accountable to each other in ways that preserve the ultimate authority of the teacher while also empowering students to speak out and act intentionally in positive ways.

The History

As Berg and Shilts recount, the idea for WOWW came from Shilts' wife Margaret sharing her concerns about some of the students she was teaching and the different challenges that they presented to her as she tried to manage the classroom and cover the curriculum. After starting in Florida, the program has been piloted in other states, including several schools we have worked with in Chicago. Later in this chapter, we will share some of our own preliminary findings on WOWW's success in helping students and teachers as well as other pilot data on WOWW we've been able to find.

The Skills

WOWW is a coaching intervention, meaning that the solution-focused practitioner operates primarily in a consultative role with the teacher and her classroom. Though the WOWW coach will be both observing the classroom and facilitating group discussions, she is never really leading a group intervention the way that many other group treatment approaches do, that is, she is not delivering a specific therapeutic intervention in a specific sequence. Right away, in WOWW, the basic tenets of SFBT are revealed in contrast to other more manualized approaches, as the clients (in this case, the teacher and her students) are put squarely in charge of setting the goals for the WOWW class discussions. Just like in other SFBT interventions, the initial session is full of questions, organized around asking the students to notice changes that have already taken place in their class. The difference as compared to a more conventional SFBT clinical session is that the WOWW coach has already observed the class and is able to share her observations directly with the class in the form of compliments, exception questions, and coping questions. This aids the eventual final task of the first WOWW session, the setting of classroom goals that relate to the learning environment. Box 4.1 shows examples of learning goals in our WOWW sessions.

BOX 4.I Phases for the WOWW Coaching Process

WOWW Program Phase

Phase 1: Observation phase
(Weeks 1–3 for an hour)

1. Introduce yourself to students, saying "I'm going to be visiting your classroom to watch for all the things the class does that are good and helpful. I will report back to you what I see."
2. Note class strengths and wait for the class to begin to point out to you their strengths, indicating their readiness for the next phase.
3. Share what you saw and prepare the class for creating classroom goals.

Phase 2: Creating Classroom Goals with Students and Teachers (Week 4 or 5)

1. With the teacher and the class, set goals for the class to work toward, for example, "show respect to each other" and ask them to scale the level of respect they have at present on a scale from 1 to 10.
2. Ask the class to describe what behavior it will take for the class to go from a "7" to an "8" or a "9" and ask the class to look for those behaviors in themselves and others over the next week.
3. Scale other goals that the class is interested in working on.

(continued)

| Phase 3: Scaling Classroom Success and Amplifying (Rest of the WOWW Sessions) | Once the scaling questions are understood, teachers may put the scaling goal on the board as a reminder and the class will be more focused on reaching the goals set for each week. Amplify the class' progress on their goals and repeat as needed. |

Source: Adapted from Berg, I. & Shilts, L. (2005). *Classroom Solutions: WOWW Coaching*. Milwaukee, WI: BFTC Press.

The WOWW coach, in our work usually the school social worker, observes the class function for a 20–30 minute period and later offers compliments and questions rooted in the SFBT framework. The class is invited to recognize their own strengths and devise solutions to class discipline problems together, rather than singling out a few defiant students. One of the major goals of WOWW coaching is to remove the tendency for classrooms with "a few" difficult students to lose cohesion and a sense of mutual purpose; by bringing the conversation back to what the whole class sees as things they want to change, the effort is made to reach out to more challenging students as well as validate the students who are already following the teacher's rules and working well with others.

The following conversation is typical of a WOWW classroom discussion, after the WOWW coach has observed and worked with the class for a few sessions. This case example comes from our work with a 3rd grade classroom:

School Social Worker (SSW): Hi everyone, my name is Mr. Kelly and I'm going to be coming to your class every week for the next couple of months. I wanted to start by getting a show of hands from all the kids here that can count to ten. Everybody? Good. Now who knows what the word "perfect" means?

Student #1: It means really, really good. So good that you can't do any better.

SSW: Good, that's it. What I want us to think about for a minute is our class here. Is this class perfect?

Students: No!! (laughter)

SSW: That's fine, no class I've visited is perfect. But what would you say the class' behavior has been in the past week, on a scale from 1 to 10, with 10 being perfect?

(SSW has students write down their score and pass them up anonymously, and he and the classroom teacher tabulate the results. During this time, the SSW has been noticing strengths in the class' behavior and asking for exceptions to the major behavior problems that the teacher has identified in class, mostly related to how the class behaves after lunch).

SSW: Thanks for voting: the class average was a 6.5, definitely not perfect, but pretty good. What do you think your class would be doing if next week your votes were an 8? What would be different and better about the behavior in this class?

Student #2: We would line up better and be able to sit in our seats after lunch more.

SSW: OK, what else?

Student #3: We would listen to our teacher the first time she says something and not make her have to raise her voice after lunch so much. (class laughs, including the teacher)

SSW: Great, what else would you need to do?

Student #4: Be nicer to each other; we yell a lot in this class sometimes after lunch.

At this point, many of the questions and approaches in the WOWW program will be familiar. As the earlier example shows, WOWW coaches are keen to ask students to first honestly assess their classroom on a particular issue (how well they listen, how well they line up, etc.) and then give themselves a scaled rating between 1 and 10. The next step the WOWW coach takes is to ask more questions from the scaling sequence to help the classroom move toward setting a goal for future classroom sessions. In the case example, students said they were at about a 6.5 in terms of their listening to the teacher when she was trying to get them organized after lunch. As the example shows, this seemingly small part of the day was actually a huge destabilizer for the afternoon, as many students failed to get on track and others said that they wished that the teacher didn't have to yell so much to get the class settled. Improving this part of the day was identified by both teachers and students as a key area to focus on, and by asking scaling questions, the WOWW coach was able to assess how much progress the class thought was realistic for the coming week.

In addition to the importance placed on getting students to mobilize around their inherent strengths, ample attention is paid to what the teacher hopes to change about her classroom. In whole-class discussions as well as debriefings with the WOWW coach after school, teachers are invited to share with the WOWW coach their perceptions of their student's behavior and their goals for change. Unlike other classroom management models that might try gimmicks or external rewards, the WOWW coaching intervention is interested in teachers and students discovering what small gains they're making and then "doing more of what's working" to turn those successes into larger gains for the whole classroom environment.

The teacher debriefing times are crucial to maximize the impact of the WOWW program. In these confidential sessions, the teacher is given the same opportunities as the students to reflect on the classroom and to identify her own capacities and strengths. Here is an example of a WOWW coach debriefing, from this same 3rd grade classroom we've discussed earlier:

School Social Worker (SSW): Thanks for meeting with me today. How's the day been?

Mrs. Smith (MS): Really good; the kids have been great. It's one of those days where you keep wondering when the other shoe's going to drop when they get back from lunch. It's almost too perfect . . .

SSW: Those kinds of days are amazing, but also a little nerve-wracking. Have you noticed anything you were doing differently this morning to help the kids be so well-behaved?

MS: No, I can't think . . . well, I did wind up singing to them this morning.

SSW: Wait, you . . . sang?

MS: Yeah, today the principal made an announcement about the class song contest for the spirit day, and I was telling the class about my favorite song, "Dancing Queen," by Abba. The kids said they never heard of it, and I told them that they needed to hear it before they got to 4th grade. Billy dared me to sing it, so I did. The kids just fell out laughing, and then they gave me a standing ovation.

SSW: You just sang, just like that?

MS: I did; I've never done that before. I mean, I like to sing with my family and at church, but I don't think the kids ever heard me sing before.

SSW: That's awesome. What makes you think that might have affected their behavior today?

MS: I'm not sure, maybe because the kids were having fun and it was only 8:15 in the morning! Or maybe they were able to see that I was in a good mood and that they could relax with me today.

SSW: What do you mean by "relaxing with you?" Are there times when you're more relaxed that you notice you get a different response from the kids?

MS: Totally. The kids totally take their cue from me; if I'm loose and having fun, we all do better together.

The Research

This approach has been piloted in Florida and Chicago over the past 3 years. In Florida, it was piloted in special education classrooms and students in the class showed increased attendance and the overall impact of the program inspired the principal to bring WOWW to regular education classrooms as well (L. Shilts, personal communication, April 18, 2007). The preliminary data from our pilot study of WOWW in Chicago follows:

> In 2006–07, the Loyola Family and Schools Partnership Program brought the Working on What Works Program ("WOWW") to three K-8 public schools in Chicago. The pilot study described here was conducted in three schools, with seven teachers who agreed to participate voluntarily.

WOWW program outcomes were measured with a pre- and posttest design completed by the participating teachers of items based on a 1-to-5 scale, assessing how teachers perceived their classroom management skills and how they perceived their students' behavior. On four of the five scales in the pre- and posttest, repeated-measure t-tests reveal that WOWW had statistically significant outcomes, indicating its effectiveness as an intervention to improve classroom climate. Those findings are summarized below:

- WOWW resulted in an increase in teacher's perception of their class as better behaved, $t(5) = 3.5$, $p < .05$, one-tailed.

- WOWW resulted in an increase in teacher's positive perception of themselves as effective classroom managers, $t(5) = 1.83$, $p < .10$, one-tailed.
- WOWW helped increase student's perception of themselves as better behaved and more respectful, $t(5) = 6.6$, $p < .05$ and $t(5) = 2.8$, $p < .05$, one-tailed.

This pilot data ($N = 6$) shows promise for WOWW emerging as an effective classroom management and staff development program. However, the small sample size and the lack of a comparison group, and the lack of information on the benefits of the WOWW program for other classroom performance variables (e.g., test scores, discipline referrals, and attendance) make it hard to say whether WOWW will have any significant impact on the many school performance variables that other classroom management techniques have claimed to address (Marzano, 2003; Wentzel, 1991).

The Future

WOWW has an intuitive appeal to school social workers trying to find positive and nonthreatening ways to help teachers and students function better together in a classroom setting. It is a promising new idea that is trying to use the active ingredients of SFBT to make meaningful impacts on classroom behavior, teacher resilience, and student achievement. It is far too early to say whether WOWW is an intervention that can positively impact such important variables in schools, though it is our hope to bring the WOWW program to more classrooms in Chicago and the surrounding suburbs during 2008 and study the program in those settings with a larger sample size and classes acting as control groups.

One major issue that has already become clear is how best to "sell" this program to schools. The initial WOWW program in Florida was explicit about making the WOWW program completely voluntary in terms of teacher participation, and we followed that same idea in our recruitment of the seven teachers who participated in our pilot study (Kelly & Bluestone-Miller, 2007, manuscript under review). However, in two of our three schools, it was clear that the principals were eager to expand the WOWW program by requiring that all teachers participate, particularly the ones that the principal thought might be burned out or even at risk of being fired. This caused challenges for our research team, as we wanted to respect the wishes of the principal while avoiding the possibility that WOWW would become another thing that was forced onto teachers' already busy plate. (We eventually were able to avoid a conflict with the principal by agreeing that we would be happy to do a larger version of the WOWW program in a future year and at that time consider the principal's wishes that the program be expanded to cover more troubled teachers.) An obvious concern we had was that WOWW not be seen as an extension of the school's teacher evaluation program, and the WOWW coach be somehow viewed as a "spy" for the principal and administrative team.

Future larger-scale implementations and evaluation of the WOWW program will have to contend with these issues, as teachers are likely to view any classroom management program that is mandatory with suspicion, and principals are likely to want to have the results of the WOWW program be available to them. This has been a problem with other teacher classroom management training programs (Marzano, 2003), and as we seek to study WOWW on a larger scale, we expect to be contending with these implementation challenges for a while to come.

Summary

Savvy school social workers have long known that one of their primary client populations in their schools is that of their teacher colleagues. The WOWW program is a teacher coaching intervention that helps school social workers target their interventions at a classroom level with the teacher and her classroom as the "client." The intervention has shown some initial positive outcomes in pilot studies, and we hope to see larger-scale WOWW studies in the coming years on WOWW's impacts on teacher classroom management styles, teacher burnout, and student variables like academic achievement and attendance. With the ever-increasing pressure on both teachers and students to be productive, we believe that school social workers need to be using classroom interventions such as WOWW to identify the strengths of classrooms and help both teachers and students work together more effectively.

5

■ ■ ■

Garza: A Solution-Building High School

Introduction

In 2007, only 4 of the 12 high schools in Austin Independent School District (AISD) in Austin, Texas, met federal standards. One of these high schools was Gonzolo Garza Independence High School, an alternative school of choice. What is surprising about this achievement is that Garza is a high school where most of the students are considered "at risk" by the school district. As an alternative school, Garza High School has many components that contribute to its overall success but a unique characteristic of Garza is that the school adopted solution-focused brief therapy (SFBT) as an integral part of its philosophy and techniques. As a solution-focused school, Garza was purposely designed to engage urban high school dropouts or students at risk of dropping out and help them complete their high school education. The developers of the solution-focused school hoped to create a setting that would enable urban youth to overcome barriers to academic success and ultimately earn credits and a high school diploma. All school administrators, teachers, and staff members were trained in SFBT techniques to aid in the engagement and work with at-risk students.

This chapter will describe a brief history of Garza High School and the training process that helped the school staff learn the solution-focused model. The chapter will also describe important characteristics of the school and further illustrate some of the solution-focused techniques used at Garza. In addition, this chapter will report the results from an outcome study that evaluated the effectiveness of the alternative school.

History of Garza High School

In 1997, the superintendent of the AISD met with Victoria Baldwin, to ask her to head a new school for juniors and seniors that removed traditional barriers to academic success found in most public high schools. With that, the creation of Gonzolo Garza Independence High School in Austin, Texas, was placed in the hands of its current principal, Victoria Baldwin. Ms. Baldwin had no office, no budget, and 5 months to create, staff and open the school in 1998. As Ms. Baldwin worked on this immense task, she started to envision the purpose of the school, the kinds of students attending the school, the situation of the world, and what she hoped the school would accomplish. Ms. Baldwin realized that the traditional high schools did not meet the needs of all students. School matters, but only insofar as it yields something that students can use, once they leave the school. She decided that the concept of Garza High School would be to prepare students with the skills necessary to meet the demands of the 21st century:

> It began with the premise of what should the graduate of the 21st century look like? What skills do they need, what is it that they need to know and be able to do? So it started with the end and worked backwards. This process of trying to figure out what the graduate of the 21st century student looked like began with brainstorming sessions involving school leaders, facilitators, parents, and students. And we designed the school program based on this information. I envisioned a school that integrated community service, social services, technology, and self-paced curriculum within a supportive campus environment.
>
> Victoria Baldwin

As Ms. Baldwin worked with others to design the school, she was very aware of the mental health and social needs of the students that she was to serve. This is why she wanted social services to become an integral part of Garza High School. Ms. Baldwin sought diligently to add more social and mental health services to the school by seeking community partners to help her, but after trying for two years, she was still not able to create the kind of comprehensive services from community helpers that she envisioned or needed to serve her students. Then in early 2000, Ms. Baldwin called on the help of a school social worker, Joann Garner, to assist her with a student with behavior problems. Joann was trained in SFBT and interviewed the student in front of Ms. Baldwin using solution-focused techniques. Joann was quickly able to develop a cooperative relationship with the student and set some goals that turned the student around. From that moment on Ms. Baldwin wanted to implement SFBT at Garza High School and asked Joann to help her achieve this goal.

Fortunately, Garza already had many characteristics that facilitated training in the solution-focused model. For example, the school was already developing a collaborative perspective between teachers, students, and parents as well as emphasizing strengths and relationships. Garza was also involved in a district-wide, dropout prevention program, known as the Impact Team, which was using solution-focused techniques to engage and assist students at risk of dropping out. The school social worker (Joann), counselors, and a few teachers at Garza were involved in the Impact Team for Garza and had training in the solution-focused approach to helping students. Through utilizing the Impact Team approach, it was possible for Ms. Baldwin and school staff to envision a broader solution-focused culture at Garza. So, Joann contacted Dr. Cynthia Franklin, one of the authors, and asked her to assist the school in learning more about SFBT.

For one year, Dr. Franklin consulted with Joann, Ms. Baldwin, and her key administrators and counselors and discussed ways to make Garza High School more solution focused. From those meetings, a plan was devised to train everyone at the school in solution-focused techniques. In most high schools, SFBT is mainly implemented by school social workers or counselors and rarely used by administrators or teachers. At Garza, however, administrators and teachers incorporated a SFBT approach into their own work and utilized key skills to lead the school. The entire school's commitment to solution-focused philosophy was key to creating a school culture where everyone buys into it and uses the techniques of SFBT. One of the Garza High School teachers said this about the training philosophy:

> It was the principal's philosophy to train the entire school for the first couple of sessions. Data clerk people were in there, registrars, custodians, because she said anyone can be an advocate. Our custodian is so involved with a lot of our kids and has been a huge advocate and role model for a lot of our kids. He does city-wide basketball and recruits some of our kids for that. He talks with them about manners and accountability, it's just amazing. Anyone can be an (advocate); a kid may bond with the cafeteria person, so that person needs to be trained like everyone else.
>
> Garza Teacher

It was clear in Ms. Baldwin's mind that she might never be able to hire enough social workers to meet all the mental health needs of her high-risk student population. So instead of trying to do so, she decided she would train all school staff to be more effective with students using the solution-focused approach. For the purposes of their work at Garza, the team of practitioners and researchers working on the design of the solution-focused school decided to call SFBT a "solution-building" approach to conversations. The term solution-building describes the use of SFBT in interviewing, which differs from the more traditional problem-solving approach (De Jong & Berg, 2008). Solution-building is an excellent approach to use with educators because it is an active, open-ended process in which students and staff construct solutions within the context of a conversation. Garza uses "solution-building conversations" that serves to assure the parties that they are not engaging in therapy. To accomplish the solution-building training for Garza High School staff, Dr. Franklin and her colleague Dr. Calvin Streeter wrote a grant to the Hogg foundation for Mental Health asking the foundation to fund the training effort. Fortunately, the Hogg Foundation for Mental Health agreed to support the training of the school staff so that they could become more solution focused, as well as paid for an additional outcome study on the school's effectiveness.

The school social worker, Joann Garner, became so involved in the training and work to transform the school into a solution-building school that she left her job as a school social worker at the AISD and joined Dr. Franklin and her team from The University of Texas at Austin, becoming Garza's main solution-focused coach. In addition, Insoo Kim Berg and Steve de Shazer, developers of the SFBT model, were also so impressed with the work of the school that they offered to adopt the school like parents adopting a child and support the training activities. From 2001 until the time of her death in 2007, Insoo visited the school frequently to conduct trainings and to consult with Ms. Baldwin and her staff. Out of the work funded by the Hogg Foundation came a detailed training manual describing Garza. An additional training video was also funded by The University of Texas. The training manual and video show how Garza became a solution-focused school and includes summaries of its transdisciplinary approach to solution-focused intervention (Franklin & Streeter, 2004). This chapter summarizes information from the Garza training manual. For more complete information about Garza High School, social workers and other professionals should review the Garza training manual that is available online at: www.utexas.edu/ssw/faculty/franklin.

How Was the School Staff Trained?

Principal Victoria Baldwin's decision to train all Garza staff in the solution-building approach presented quite a challenge for training. Ms. Baldwin's forthright character and determination, however, were directed toward this task. Ms. Baldwin displays a sign in her office that reads, "Show Me the Money," so there was never much doubt about the fact that she wanted the job completed. In November 2001, the first training was a half-day of professional development for Garza staff. From that time on the training evolved so that the teachers, called facilitators at Garza, assumed ownership of the process and became more involved in designing and delivering the training. Several strategies were developed by the teachers (facilitators) and research team that helped facilitate learning of the solution-focused philosophy and techniques including the following:

1. A library of solution-focused resources was made available to teachers (facilitators).
2. Teachers (facilitators) organized themselves into groups and formed a book club of readings and exchanged ideas about the readings.
3. Brown bag meetings were set for teachers and others to watch video tapes of solution-focused interventions.
4. In-service trainings were organized with Insoo Kim Berg serving as the trainer. Insoo also met with smaller groups such as the principal, administrators and counselors for additional training and consultation.
5. A solution-focused coach worked inside the school and was available for classroom consultations and modeling of the solution-focused approach.
6. Teachers (facilitators) and other staff were provided quick reference sheets for solution-focused techniques they could use with students.
7. Principal Baldwin added competencies in solution-focused intervention to her annual performance evaluation with staff.

The experience gained from training Garza High School staff in solution-focused techniques also revealed several strategies that other schools can employ when introducing the solution-focused approach to a school. Some of these ideas include the following:

1. Determining the overall readiness of a campus to learn the model.
2. Creating specific learning steps in a training process such as first teaching the philosophy of solution-building and then building in the steps to facilitate the learning and application of specific techniques.
3. Making use of the solution-building coach for the school.
4. Adding solution-building philosophy and techniques in forms used in the school.
5. Forging partnerships with administrators, counselors and teachers. Box 5.1 suggests other steps to follow when introducing the solution-focused approach to a school.

BOX 5.1 Training Steps for Schools

- Obtain support from administration
- Identify one person to be primarily responsible for training and adherence
- Create strong partnerships with selected school staff
- Assess what the school is already doing to build solutions
- Introduce the model through an interdisciplinary team structure
- Seek input from all constituents, especially students
- Maintain a school focus in solution-building conversations
- Provide opportunities for training by an expert in solution-focused therapy
- Supporting educators in shaping the model with their own unique philosophy and approach

Source: Franklin, C., & Streeter, C. L. (2004), *Solution-focused accountability schools for the 21st century*. Austin: The Hogg Foundation for Mental Health, The University of Texas at Austin.

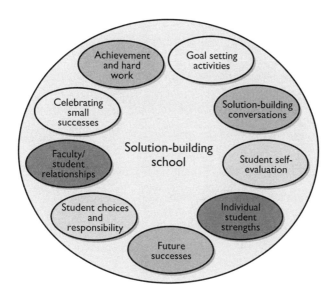

FIGURE 5.1. Characteristics of a solution-building school.

It is also important to acknowledge that throughout the training process, a sharing across professional lines defined the emergence of solution-building at Garza. School social workers, counselors, teachers, and administrators learned a new approach to help and educate students and melded their areas of expertise into a unique application of solution-building. In such an approach, the different team members share their knowledge and expertise with one another and create new methods for intervention by adapting knowledge from one another. Streeter and Franklin (2002) call this learning across disciplinary boundaries a transdisciplinary team approach to solving problems. It is also important to note that the students were a part of the team effort in developing approaches at Garza. As a solution-building school, listening to students and taking their suggestions is a part of the culture at Garza. Figure 5.1 describes other solution-focused characteristics of Garza.

Who Are the Students at Garza High School?

Students at Garza are a diverse group who reflect the Austin community at large. When Garza first opened its doors in 1998, it had 292 students and the student body's ethnic composition consisted of 25% African American, 30% Caucasian, and 45% Hispanic students. At the end of the 2005–2006 school year, Garza had around 300 students with 11% African American students, 53% Caucasian students, and 36% Hispanic students (Garza High School, 2006). Some of the characteristics of students attracted to Garza include the following:

- Students who will profit and thrive from a nontraditional approach to learning characterized by an integrated, interdisciplinary curriculum that is problem and project based and enhanced by access to technology
- Students who wish to pursue a high school education as part of a comprehensive program, including preparation for postsecondary education and a strong school-to-career component, as well as integrated health and social services
- Students who need support and encouragement in a personalized learning environment
- Students who have the motivation and ability to learn independently and wish to accelerate learning
- Students who have a need for a flexible schedule that is personalized and individualized
- Students who have experienced life circumstances that have presented barriers to their graduation
- Students who have dropped out or are likely to drop out of a regular high school program
- Students who have already earned 10 credits
- Students who are pregnant or are teen parents and need child care
- Students who find themselves lost in a large high school and lack a significant attachment in the traditional high school setting resulting in poor academic performance with subsequent loss of graduation credit

Interviews at Garza with a sample group of their students and further examination of school records indicated that many of the students at Garza had experienced multiple hardships such as homelessness, violence, substance abuse, and mental health challenges. According to the 2006 Texas Education Agency (TEA) Accountability Report, 76% of Garza students are identified as at-risk. Recently, the student demographics indicate a shift in student enrollment with more Caucasian students applying whereas applications by African American and Hispanic students are decreasing.

Garza's Curriculum and Instruction Approach

The goal of the curriculum at Garza is thematic, interdisciplinary, and problem and project based. Using the most current best practices in education, Garza High School empowers students to become life-long learners and productive members of society. Consistent with the school's solution-focused approach, the curriculum is self-paced and portfolio driven, which allows for each student to set individual goals for achieving their educational progress. The self-paced format of the curriculum demands independent decision-making, time management, self-motivation, and acceptance of personal responsibility in success or failure. Consistent with solution-focused techniques, the curriculum also makes use of the intrinsic motivation of students by incorporating student interests through integration of subjects resulting in multicredit courses, service learning, and practical skill building in the real world. One of the popular integrative, multicredit courses, for example, is Crime Scene Investigation (CSI) that integrates government and criminal justice information into a practical experience working with the Austin Police Department in the area of forensics.

In addition, the curriculum links what happens in the classroom with the real-life situations relevant to careers and postsecondary opportunities. Students participate in the Early Start program, for example, that allows them to earn credits at a local community college. Students are further introduced to the world of work through internships, apprenticeships, and jobs within the business community, preparing them to take their place in the work force. For example, Garza's horticulture class developed a business called Garza Gardens, which grows herbs and vegetables on campus and then sells them at the weekly farmers market. The goals of this program, which is student operated, are to learn about horticulture and the ecosystem, introduce agribusiness marketing and management to the students, and also help beautify the campus.

Shaping Educational Progress

Complimenting small steps toward one's educational goals are a part of the solution-focused philosophy and techniques. The practical, self-paced and goal-directed emphasis of the curriculum at Garza High School provides many opportunities to reward and compliment incremental successes of students and to build confidence in their academic skills and abilities. One of the attributes of the school, for example, is to shape learning through helping students achieve small successes. From the very beginning of their educational experience at Garza, students learn what they are good at doing and are able to confidently articulate their individual strengths and future goals.

The ideas of strengths, goal setting, and future goals are introduced, for example, in the student's orientation to the school known as Blue Prints. The results of this approach can be observed in the behaviors of the school's graduates. Simply ask a Garza graduate what they are good at doing and what their future goals are and most can answer these questions without hesitation. For example, Cynthia Franklin recently did a presentation on SFBT at the Ann Richards School for Young Leaders with a recent Garza graduate, Angelo McHorse.

Angelo is an American Indian originally from Taos, New Mexico, Pueblo. Angelo impressed upon the audience, including Dr. Franklin, with his experiential knowledge of the solution-focused approach and confident ways that he personally benefited from this approach to education. Before attending Garza High School, Angelo was on his way to becoming a high school dropout. Now, he is a recent high school graduate who was also able to describe his skills and goals. He stated, for example, that he was good at seeing the diverse elements of a situation and making a difference to the environment. His specific future goal was to gain postsecondary education leading to an engineering degree that focused on the ecological environment.

The Star Walk

One of Garza's most innovative and solution-focused initiatives is the Star Walk, which is an individual graduation ceremony that is orchestrated for each student when they finish all of their high school credits. Since the school is self-paced, the students finish high school at different times during a school year and this is cause for a celebration of that student's achievements, which is acknowledged through the "Star Walk." The "Star Walk" serves as a ritual rite of passage for each student and is celebrated with his or her closest family, friends, teachers, and fellow students.

There are three components to this celebratory event:

1. A presentation of the student's completed academic portfolio before teachers, family, and friends. The portfolio presentation allows the students to discuss their academic skills and successes and show samples of their work to attendees.

Some of the student's teachers also participate by reading letters of reference and endorsements about the student's character and academic abilities.

2. The principle endorsements and presentation of the Garza Star, which is an inscribed glass emblem, like a paper weight, that is presented to each graduate of the school in a ceremonial manner. At this presentation, the principal also tells an inspiring story, like a testimonial, about how much the student has changed since he/she came to Garza and highlights his/her success in the school. Included in this testimonial are statements about the positive character traits (e.g., persistence, hard working, generosity, determination, etc.) of the student and a list of the student's future goals.

3. The march around the school with selected family members, friends, and teachers with accompanying music played over the campus speakers. During this march, the other students and teachers come out into the hall or stand in the doors of classrooms to applaud, cheer, and blow bubbles.

The Use of Technology in Curriculum

It is the philosophy of solution-focused therapy to help people recognize and use their personal strengths and resources, and to make use of other resources they need to succeed in life. Consistent with this strengths-based philosophy, Garza High School prides itself on being a highly resourced, 21st century school by incorporating different technologies into the student learning environment. The principal, Victoria Baldwin's goals for the school were for it to be both high tech and high touch in its approach to learning. Of course, the use of technology per se is not a solution-focused strategy but it is integrally important to skill building and success of the students. By integrating technology with the curriculum, the classes foster critical thinking, solution-building, and project-based learning. Consistent with the solution-focused techniques, Garza's technology focus provides numerous options for learning and a sense of hope and destiny to students who are ready to give up or have already given up the chance to earn a high school diploma.

Garza has been highly successful in its use of technologies and that is why the U.S. Department of Education honored Garza by selecting it as being one of the top 100 wired schools in America. Technology tools available in every classroom include: multimedia computers with Internet connections, printers, and a variety of software. In addition, scanners, video cameras, digital cameras, audio recorders, projectors, and graphic tablets are readily available. Beyond equity of access to technological equipment, students have a variety of technology courses to choose from like computer applications and maintenance, desktop publishing, multimedia animation, media technology, and web mastering. As a result, all of Garza's courses integrate technology and students receive multiple opportunities to explore and expand their technology skills and link the curriculum with real-life situations relevant to careers and postsecondary opportunities. Garza students, for example, have opportunities to learn how to produce and edit media products such as DVDs. The students have won numerous state awards in Texas, competing against other high schools, for their skills in the media area.

Important School Characteristics

It is important to discuss the fact that Garza incorporates many attributes from the research literature on what constitutes an effective school and drop-out prevention program. The characteristics did not come from the SFBT model but they are highly congruent with the model's underlying assumptions and techniques. A few of the important characteristics of Garza are described here and readers are directed to the training manual developed by Franklin and Streeter (2004) for a more detailed exploration of Garza and its educational programs.

1. The strong presence and leadership style of the principal has been suggested as an important component of effective schools and alternative schools (Mendez-Morse, 1992; Reynolds, 2001). Strong leadership helps create stability in the school environment and, in the case of Garza, encourages teachers and staff to utilize the solution-building model in their work. Davis and Osborn (2000) states, for example, that a solution-focused school cannot operate without the principal's full endorsement and active participation. Although some school administrators support and encourage the use of solution-building by school social workers, few actually practice these techniques in their own daily duties. Administrators at Garza lead by example and

constantly use solution-building techniques with students, facilitators, and staff.

2. Positive student relationships, including a low teacher-student ratio for classes (Van Heusden, 2000; Waxman, Anderson, Huang, & Weinstein, 1997). Solution-building is a very relationship-oriented approach focusing on collaborative relationships between students and staff. The smaller classroom environment makes it possible to form these personal relationships, as well as individualized attention and educational solutions for students.

3. Use of alternative school approach to dropout prevention. Although the research is limited, alternative schools have been cited as being one of the most effective ways to graduate students who are dropout prone (Reimer & Cash, 2003). Dupper (2006) describes two opposing models of alternative schools. One model is disciplinary or correctional in nature designed to fix problem students and the second is academic and creative in nature promoting a more effective way to educate students. Garza offers the second approach creating an alternative school program that is challenging, caring, and supportive. The Garza approach is consistent with other academic alternative school programs that are designed to help students with diverse learning styles and backgrounds succeed. Staffs in this type of alternative schools are working in this setting by choice and are dedicated to helping students with diverse learning styles take responsibility for their own learning. Curriculum and instruction within these types of alternative schools offers learning that is individualized, engaging, and relevant. The academic alternative school by design is a school of choice like Garza and fosters a full instructional program from a multidisciplinary team.

Garza as a Solution-Building School

As described previously, Garza High School started evolving into a solution-building high school during the summer of 2000 when the administrators, school social worker, and a group of teachers and staff began incorporating SFBT techniques and ideas in their work with at-risk students. It is important to note that the solution-building approach was not forced on school administrators, staff, and faculty. Instead, it evolved out of their intrinsic work with student motivation and behavior around their mutual interest in dropout prevention. Solution-building, essentially, became a philosophy guiding their success with at-risk students and represented the primary intervention model undergirding their school mental health practices.

Solution-Building Skills and Techniques

This strengths-based philosophy emphasizes choosing hopeful, positive, empowering language, experimenting with new behavior and celebrating incremental change. The assumptions, values, and beliefs that inform SFBT in school settings can be grouped into four constellations of concepts as outlined by Murphy (1997) and Thomas (1997):

Solution Driven:
- The purpose of the conversation is to discover clues to a possible course of action that will reduce the severity of the problem.
- A small change in any aspect of the difficulty can create a solution.
- Complex problems do not need complex solutions, nor is there a logical connection between the problem and the solution.
- Successful solutions are conceived in terms of taking new action rather than stopping old behaviors.

Asset Based:
- Students, teachers, and parents have the strengths and abilities to change school difficulties.
- Any goal must be developed by the person experiencing the difficulty.
- Recognizing and affirming the student's competence and ability to change is highly motivating.

Focus Shift:
- Concentration on future possibilities supports change.
- Insight into the nature of the problem is not necessary for building solutions.
- There is always an exception to the difficulty, a time or place when the problem was less or even absent.

- In a school setting, the emphasis is upon solutions that enhance personal development, academic success, and progress toward graduation.

Experimental Action:
- Change is going to happen.
- There is no one correct course of action toward building a solution.
- There are many possible meanings and ways to understand any given behavior; therefore, if one view is not working, try another.
- If it works do more of it; if it does not work, do something else.

These assumptions demonstrate how solution-building shifts away from the past and toward the future and differs from problem-solving talk. Box 5.2 illustrates the differences between the problem-solving approach and the solution-building process. Furthermore, there is minimal attention paid to what is wrong. Attention is focused on what is working and looking for

---

BOX 5.2 Comparing Solution Building With Problem Solving

SOLUTION BUILDING	PROBLEM SOLVING
"How did you do that?"	"Why did you do that?"
Focus on future	Emphasis on past
Solution-talk	Problem-talk
Attention on what is working	Attention on what is wrong
Student is capable	Student is flawed
Student is source of solution	Teacher is source of solution
Teacher skilled at "not knowing"	Teacher is "all knowing"
Frees teacher from responsibility of fixing the problem	Teacher accepts responsibility for fixing the problem

Source: Greene, R. (Ed.). *Risk and resiliency in social work practice* (p. 124). Belmont, CA: Brooks/Cole Johnny.

---

exceptions to the problem (Berg, 1994). The student is seen as capable, not flawed. The entire endeavor is being hopeful and places responsibility for the change on the student experiencing the difficulty. Educators can easily learn to use this system of positive skills to aid students in discovering their own strengths and building solutions based on these strengths and abilities.

Garza's administrators and teachers use the solution-building model to lead the school and facilitate positive relationships with students. They view the students as the experts in identifying their own solutions to their problems, which is an approach different from the usual expert-driven strategies. Because Garza's administrators and teachers believe students have the knowledge and capabilities to solve their own problems, student input is valued and sought out. Here are some of the ways that Garza's administrators and teachers use the solution-building intervention skills to assist students:

- Helping students come up with a realistic solution
- Looking for ways in which the solution is already occurring in their lives
- Determining small, measurable goals toward the solution
- Taking immediate steps to make a difference in educational and life outcomes.

This strengths-based approach is a major theme throughout the solution-building school and SFBT offers all administrators and teachers specific skills for fostering strengths in students. Identifying the student's strengths helps build confidence in a student that a solution is possible and empowers the student to continue building on his or her strengths. This helps create positive changes for the students quickly and shifts the focus away from the negatives.

School Applications of SFBT

For Garza, there is no doubt that the foundation of the solution-building school rests on the shoulders of the teachers. In order for a school to maximize its potential as a solution-building school, it becomes important for all participants in the school to be able to live out the model. Solution-building occurs when a conversation is based on certain communication strategies. Choosing positive and hopeful language, creating a vision for the future without problems, and identifying goals and steps toward goals are techniques that advance the movement toward a solution.

One early hurdle to clear in helping the diverse staff in a school use SFBT is the discomfort administrators and teachers sometimes feel about the idea of using techniques from a therapy approach. Educators do not want to be told to act like social workers or counselors. In some circumstances, school social workers and counselors may not be too approving of the idea because of fear of violation of professional boundaries (Gutkin & Curtis, 1999). One way to approach this resistance with varying parties is to analogize the use of solution-building by diverse school staff to the concept of first aid. Anyone who sees another person hurt can render basic first aid. First aid and triage involve assessing the extent of injury and discomfort, stabilizing the situation, determining the level of care needed, and either providing the necessary care or aiding in accessing what they require. Garza administrators and teachers do render mental health first aid and triage. They provide mental health first aid when a student is obviously distressed, and they determine the level of care and intervention the student requires, which usually involves referrals to the school social worker or another member of the student support team (e.g., counselor). In providing first aid, teachers listen to the student, review what is going right, and negotiate some goal-directed next steps. The discussion below, between Ms. Wilson (teacher) and Liz (student), offers an example of first aid:

Liz (obviously upset and angry): Why did you call my mother? She has been ragging me constantly and demanding that I come home where she can make me go to school.

Ms. Wilson: Liz, let's step out in the hall. Now, can you tell me what has upset you so?

Liz: (starting to cry) I don't live at home. My stepfather kicked me out at Thanksgiving after I had a fight with my mother. She hit me and called me a whore. They both drink a lot. I love my mom, but I just can't be there right now.

Ms. Wilson: I'm really sorry you are having all these problems, Liz. You really do well when you make it to class. Aren't you trying to graduate in May?

Liz: Yeah, that's the idea, but I also need to get more hours at work. My girl friend's mother has been nice, but I feel I need to help more.

Ms. Wilson: Mr. Castro might be able to help you with the work problem. You could go this afternoon to talk to him. But we still need to talk about what will help about attendance.

Liz: I guess I just can't be absent ever again.

Ms. Wilson: I don't ask for perfection. And, anyway, you've got so much going on in your life. But you know I have to keep up with my students' attendance. I certainly don't want to get you in trouble with your mother, but I have to call after you have been absent. Your mother's is the only number I have.

Liz: I really don't want you calling my mother or my friend's house.

Ms. Wilson: What do you think I could do instead?

Liz: Well, if I'm not going to make it, I could call you.

Ms. Wilson: I'm certainly willing to try that. But if you're out two days and you haven't called I'll have to call someone. Who do you want me to call?

Liz: You can call me at my friend's house. The number is 751–1890.

Franklin & Streeter, 2004, p. 251

Often, students like Liz can be helped to get back to class and their schooling fairly quickly. Other students have needs beyond first aid, and the teacher's role is to help them connect with the school social worker or other mental health professional at school who can work more intensively with the student and provide referrals to community resources.

As mentioned earlier, three key solution-building techniques used by Garza administrators and teachers are identifying strengths, looking for solutions, and looking for exceptions. These techniques are used by staff, teachers, and students on a regular basis for a number of different situations. Building on the guiding principles for a solution-building school mentioned in Chapter 2, administrators and teachers incorporate these solution-building techniques in their daily roles.

Solution-Building Skill: Identifying Strengths

One of the key ways in which administrators and teachers can use solution-building in their work with students is by focusing on strengths. This can be especially effective when working with students who are experiencing problems or exhibiting behavioral issues. It is a different way of thinking about the helping process because solution-building assumes that students have the inherent strengths and resources to help themselves. By focusing on the student's strengths rather than their problems, change can occur more rapidly (Lipchik, 2002). The following is a case example where the principal (Mr. Juliano) uses solution-building with a student (Nathan) who has been in a residential treatment center for substance abuse and returns to school:

Nathan: Hi Mr. Juliano, I just wanted to stop by to let you know I'm back from my treatment.

Mr. Juliano: It's good to see you and I'm glad you're back.

Nathan: It's good to be back but it does feel a little weird. I haven't felt a lot of these emotions in a long time. Before when I was drinking and smoking pot, I just didn't care about anything and was just depressed.

Mr. Juliano: Now you can see the difference between when you're clean and sober and when you're not. You look and sound a lot better than the last time we met. I can see you've been working hard to get better and that your determination is a real strength.

Nathan: Yeah, I do notice a difference and I've been working hard to keep clean.

Mr. Juliano: Could you tell me how you've been able to do that?

Nathan: Well, for one, I stopped hanging out with my old buddies who still use. I also try to focus more on my school work and go to the gym.

Mr. Juliano: Nathan, it sounds like you're really working hard to take better care of yourself both academically and physically. What else can we do here or what can I do to help you stay clean and sober?

By focusing on strengths rather than problems, the principal reinforces the point that this student has the skills and knowledge to succeed and gives the student credit for that success. This builds confidence that a solution is possible and empowers the student to continue building on his or her strengths. It helps to form responsibility and helps students understand that they can work through difficult scenarios even if they don't like them (Murphy, 1997).

Solution-Building Skill: Looking for Solutions

Along with identifying strengths, a second major component of solution-building focuses on looking for solutions. In solution-focus brief therapy, it's the use of language that helps bring about changes for the client. The phrasing of questions is presumed to affect the way clients view their problems and the potential for change (Cade & O'Hanlon, 1993). Behavioral change occurs by working with the student to identify the problem, to look for times when the problem is absent, and to develop attainable goals to help resolve the problem (Sklare, 1997). The administrators and teachers use Socratic questioning to help the student view the situation from a different perspective and to look for clues where the solution is already occurring in the student's life. Socratic questioning involves asking questions that steers clients to discovering answers to their own problems through collaborative exploration between client and practitioner (Overholser, 1993).

Even when disciplining students, administration takes a solution-building approach, and perhaps this contributes to why they have so few disciplinary referrals. Violence is almost absent in the school's history, for example with only two fights occurring between students since the school's opening in 1998. When students are given detention, they are required not only to think about what they did to get into trouble but also to explore what they could have done differently. They are asked to envision what a solution would look like and how they can make those changes.

> During detention students are given a thought sheet that is used to help students write out what happened. We would ask specific questions like what happened the first time, what happened the second time, what could you have done to keep that from happening, what will you do the next time this happens? And so that was a way for us not to have to sit there with them but still engaged them in some mental reflection about what happened. So it became, what can we do to do a better job? What could you have done for this not to happen? What were some of the other choices you could have made? What can you do to correct that? So the kids would rattle off solutions to those questions for you because they know the right answers.
>
> Sam Watson
> Assistant Principal

Solution-building requires that the individual concentrate on the present and the future. Because the past cannot be changed, it is not necessary to analyze past actions that resulted in the problem in order to find a solution to the problem. Solution-building emphasizes that change is constant and inevitable; a small change can lead to bigger changes. By working with students to find solutions in a situation where the student feels stuck or overwhelmed, making a small step toward the goal can generate hope and lead to bigger changes (Lipchik, 2002).

Solution-Building Skill: Looking for Exceptions

Looking into the past to seek exceptions to the problem is quite different from scouring the past for multiple details about the origin and reasons for unwanted behavior and feelings. Teachers at Garza have found the practice of looking for exceptions to problems helpful in their conversations with students. Shifting the focus to those times when the unproductive behavior did not happen provides teachers with valuable information and may even furnish clues to changes they might want to make in individual assignments. Below is an example of how looking for exceptions can help shift the focus away from a student's unproductive behavior during a case consultation with a school social worker.

Teacher: I have tried to listen and be understanding, but Alice continues to spend most of her class time surfing the web instead of writing her history report. I don't know why she insists on doing this.

Coach: I don't know why either. Was there any time this week that you noticed she was working on her class assignment?

Teacher: (After a long pause) You know, she did some work on her report Tuesday morning.

Coach: What was different about Tuesday morning?

Teacher: She found a web site about fashion in the roaring twenties. She's doing her report on that era. I could tell she was really interested in the flapper and her style. She asked me if I thought there were any books in the library.

Coach: Can you think of any other times when she's been that engaged in researching her report?

Teacher: She had a lot of questions when another student presented a report on the life of the pioneer woman. Alice was more animated than I've seen her since the first of the year. There may have been some other times, too.

Coach: Well, if you see a pattern to those exceptions you could come up with a way to alter the assignment and capture that interest and animation.

Teacher: I know there have been other times when she showed that excitement. I'll have to do some thinking about this.

Franklin & Streeter, 2004, p. 246

These examples of solution-building techniques used by administrators, teachers, and school social workers can be easily incorporated into other aspects of their roles because of its flexibility. The ideas of identifying strengths, looking for small, measurable solutions, and seeking exceptions to the problem are skills that can be used by anyone in most situations.

Research on Garza

As discussed in Chapter 3, the research indicates that SFBT is a promising and useful approach in working with at-risk students in a school setting. Specifically, the studies that have been completed suggest that SFBT is beneficial in helping students reach their goals, alleviate their concerns, reduce the intensity of their negative feelings, raise their self-esteem, manage their conduct problems, and increase their grades (Corcoran & Stephenson, 2000; Franklin, Biever, Moore, Clemons, & Scamardo, 2001; LaFountain & Garner, 1996; Littrell, Malia, & Vanderwood, 1995; Newsome, 2004; Springer, Lynch, & Rubin, 2000). Because of the promising results from these studies, the Franklin, Streeter, Kim, and Tripodi (2007) believed that a solution-building school would be effective for students who dropped out of their prior high school or were at risk of dropping out of school. Therefore, a quasi-experimental research study was conducted to see how effective Garza's solution-building approach was at helping at-risk students meet their academic goals. Franklin et al. (2007) assessed the effectiveness of Garza High School in terms of credits earned, attendance, and graduation rates. Furthermore, the researchers anticipated that the results might help inform an effective model for dropout prevention and building on the evidence-based literature for schools dealing with students at risk of dropping out of school.

The experimental group, from Garza High School, consisted of 46 students whereas the comparison group consisted of 39 students from a traditional public high school in the same urban area where many of the Garza students had previously attended. Participants from the comparison high school were recruited from a list provided by AISD. Students from the comparison group were selected because they were statistically matched with the Garza sample on the following characteristics: attendance, number of credits earned, graduation rate, participation in the free lunch program, race, gender, and whether the student is defined as being "at risk" according to Texas Education Code criteria.

Data for credits earned was obtained from the AISD. The credits earned variable (credits earned divided by credits attempted) was computed for each of four consecutive semesters beginning with the Fall 2002 semester and continuing through the Spring 2004 semester. These four semesters were chosen for the analysis because most students in the Garza sample entered Garza just before the start of the 2003–2004 academic year. If Garza is effective in helping students earn more credits (as a proportion of credits attempted) that change should be most apparent between the Spring 2003 and Fall 2003 semesters.

Similarly, data for attendance was obtained from AISD and included two sources of information related to attendance: days attended and calendar days (number of school days). Data is available for each fall and spring semester beginning in 2002 through 2004. A new variable was computed that shows days attended as a proportion of school days for the semester. This variable represents the proportion of school days that the student actually attended.

A statistical test known as repeated measures analysis of variance (ANOVA) found that over time, there was change in the number of credits earned as a proportion of credits attempted for both the Garza sample and the comparison sample. Although both groups increased their proportion of credits earned, independent samples t-tests showed the Garza sample had statistically significant higher average proportion of credits earned to credits attempted than the comparison sample.

A repeated measures ANOVA was also conducted to examine differences between groups on the attendance variable. Independent samples t-test also showed that differences between the two groups on attendance was statistically significant and favored the comparison group. Although both groups show a decrease in the attendance mean per semester, the comparison group shows a higher proportion of school days attended to school days for the semester. That is, the students at the comparison school did better than the students at Garza in terms of attending classes.

One possible explanation why Garza students did not have consistent attendance lies in the unique curriculum design of the school. In a regular high school, such as our comparison school, students can be seriously penalized academically for not attending class. At Garza, because of its self-paced content mastery curriculum, students can work at their own pace. This means that students who understand the course material well can complete their course requirements faster and finish before the school semester is officially over. This might explain why the Garza sample's mean attendance rate was low for the spring semester of 2004. These Garza students, who were seniors at the time, could have finished their course work before the traditional semester was over and therefore would not need to attend classes anymore. The AISD, however, counts the missed days in their database, and considers these students absent. The self-paced curriculum allows a student to come into the school and work very hard for concentrated periods of time to master the content. Therefore, the relationship between attendance and performance is mitigated by the nature of the curriculum (Franklin et al., 2007). A follow-up statistical analysis correlating attendance with credits earned confirmed that there was no relationship between attendance and credits earned at Garza, suggesting that this explanation may be correct. School data from a 2007 report suggests that Garza found a way to address their attendance issues so that they could meet school district and federal standards. According to Principal Baldwin, her student advisory group helps develop the solution.

To assess the graduation rate for the 2003–2004 academic year, data on all students who were classified as being in the 12th grade in the spring semester of 2004 was used. Data from AISD indicated that there were 67 students classified as 12th graders in spring 2004—37 from the Garza sample and 30 from the comparison sample. Of the 37 students from the Garza sample, 23 (62%) graduated in 2004. In the comparison sample, we see that 27 (90%) of the 12th graders graduated. The comparison sample had a higher graduation rate than the Garza sample when using a cohort graduation rate set by the No Child Left Behind policy (students need to graduate in 4 years).

An analysis of the 14 students in the Garza sample who did not graduate found that only two students had dropped out of school. Nine of the other students were still enrolled at Garza, two were enrolled in a GED program, and one was being home schooled. Although Garza's graduation rate is lower than the comparison sample, the fact that 12 of the 14 students are still in some kind of academic program is significant for public schools because of their goals of educating every student. It is important that the at-risk students at Garza were still working toward their high school proficiency and were able to catch up on their academic credits. In addition, of the 23 students in the Garza sample who graduated in 2004, 12 (52%) have enrolled in some kind of postsecondary education program, which is even more significant for the success of the school's graduates

The study by Franklin et al. (2007) suggests that in order to truly "leave no child behind" urban high schools need more social services and mental health resources to help remove the barriers to learning. The good news from this study is that when schools are organized like Garza, it becomes possible for teachers and administrators to be trained to serve as the first line of defense in this mental health effort. The collaborative model of SFBT encourages teachers and administrators to learn skills and the resources to work as partners with school social workers and other mental health professionals to provide more support for students.

Follow-Up Study

Even though the researchers were not able to do a follow-up study on Garza, the school district and state education agency have continued to collect data on the school's performance. According to the latest data from the Texas Education Agency (2006), 76% of Garza students from the class of 2005 were classified as "at-risk" but still the class of 2005 had a 98% completion rate, which is similar to the 2004 class and a dropout rate of 1.2%. Garza students also ranked first in terms of highest average SAT scores out of AISD's 12 high schools and 86% of graduates indicated pursuing higher education during the 2005–2006 school year. In addition, Garza has been recognized as the Best Public School and Program Model by the Austin Chronicle, Advanced Micro Devices Corporation, World Congress Informational Technology, and as an exemplary school by American Youth Policy Forum for Youth Development and Policy Research (Garza High School, 2006). The school has also won the high school teacher of the year award for the Austin district twice in its brief history. These are just some of the accolades and awards Garza has received over the past 5 years, which further support the school's success at reaching out to students who were at risk of dropping out.

The Future

Garza Independence High School has developed a unique solution-focused, school culture that helps students change their beliefs and relationships. Garza shows that administrators and teachers can learn and apply the principles inherent in the solution-building approach such as focusing on individual strengths, goal setting, looking for exceptions, and identifying solutions. Garza serves as a model program for how a public alternative school makes the paradigm shift to a strengths-based focus and uses the behavior change procedures offered by the SFBT approach.

By using the solution-building approach, Garza became a place that provides emotional and social support and engages students who have limited support and help in their neighborhood, families, and friends. This type of social support and individualized attention appears to be critical for the retention and graduation of some at-risk students. Many youths who fail or leave urban high schools prematurely have complex lives where they have many issues to cope with such as substance abuse, loss and crisis, abuse, poverty, mental health problems, and family conflict. Research has indicated that family problems, mental health, and substance abuse issues are associated with high school dropouts (Aloise-young & Chavez, 2002; Jordan, Lara, & McPartland, 1996; Rumberger & Thomas, 2000). High schools may experience the greatest severity of problems because of the developmental issues confronting adolescence, and the worsening over time of unresolved problems. It is unlikely that high schools will be able to be successful at graduating all students without strategies for assisting students with these complex issues. It is possible for school districts to learn from the success of Garza and develop their own solution-focused alternative schools that may improve their success with at-risk students.

Summary

This chapter described the brief history of a solution-focused, public alternative high school called Gonzolo Garza Independence High School in Austin, Texas. Major solution-focused techniques employed by the school staff include identifying strengths, looking for small, measurable solutions, and seeking exceptions to the problem. These are skills that can be used, in most situations, by the entire staff, who undergo extensive training.

An outcome study that evaluated the effectiveness of Garza High School compared students from Garza with students from another Austin high school with similar characteristics and found Garza students earned significantly more credits over time than the Austin students. In addition, 52% of the students that participated in the study on Garza have enrolled in some kind of postsecondary education program.

The study also explained why attendance rates and time to receive a diploma may not be the best measure of outcome when a school is using a mastery-based, self-paced curriculum. A strength of an alternative school like Garza is that it is able to engage students over time, and help them graduate.

Over the past 5 years, Garza has won many local and national awards as a model dropout prevention program and continues to demonstrate excellent academic outcomes, while graduating the majority of its students.

6

■ ■ ■

SFBT in Action: Case Examples of School Social Workers Using SFBT

Through a series of five case studies, school social workers show how they adapted solution-focused brief therapy (SFBT) to their school contexts. Using a variety of treatment modalities (family, small group, and macropractice), these school social workers show how flexible and powerful SFBT ideas can be in a school setting.

Ultimately, the research on SFBT in schools can only give so much direction, context, and inspiration. On the basis of the feedback we have got teaching SFBT ideas to school social workers, we know that school social workers need and want to hear how others have "done it" and adapted SFBT to their own school social work practices. This chapter will offer a series of brief case studies where school social workers:

1. use SFBT techniques to change the direction of a case study evaluation meeting to focus more on student and family strengths;
2. lead a session of SFBT family therapy led by a school social worker in a school-based mental health clinic;
3. conduct SFBT group treatment for students struggling with anxiety;
4. map out a solution-focused needs assessment that helped a school social worker create a family health and employment fair in an impoverished community;

5. organize and conduct an 8-week SFBT group session for grandparents raising grandchildren (GRGs), drawing on grandparents' "old-school wisdom" for raising their grandchildren (Newsome & Kelly, 2004).

Where it is available, we will provide additional resources for SFBT school social workers to find more information on how they can adopt these practice ideas themselves. Though key identifying information about the schools have been changed to protect confidentiality, all of these case examples are based on real practitioners' work, and they show how SFBT can incorporate these ideas into their school social work practice.

A Solution-Focused Case Study Process

School social workers nationwide often participate in case study evaluations (Gleason, 2007; Watkins & Kurtz, 2001) to discern eligibility for special education placement and services. These evaluations are based on diagnostic criteria outlined in the Individuals with Disabilities Education Improvement Act (IDEA) rules and regulations (Altshuler & Kopels, 2003; Constable, 2006) and reflect a deficit model common to diagnostic criteria in special education and the medical model (Gleason, 2007; House, 2002). This case example will show how a school social worker used the ideas of resilience and the strengths perspective in SFBT to conduct a routine case study evaluation.

Jenny (name changed for confidentiality) was practicing in her elementary school for 5 years when she decided to do something different with her special education evaluations. For years, she had been the person to speak after the classroom teacher and the nurse had given their reports, and before the school psychologist shared the results of her testing. Most of the reports she gave tried gamely to focus on the student's strengths and capacities for succeeding in both regular and special education, but something seemed to fall flat. The clinical and family information she was collecting focused primarily on what was not working with the student and his or her family, and though she tried to soften the more diagnostic language inherent in assessing child and family functioning, she wondered whether families heard any of the strengths she was presenting, or just heard words like "deficits" and "disorder" instead. Working as a white school social worker with a majority African American student population, she also worried about the tendency of her special education team to focus on family and student problems rather than any of the family system's strengths.

After attending some SFBT trainings offered by the Loyola Family and School Partnerships Program (FSPP), she learned of two rating scales that might help her fulfill her report-writing responsibilities and also move the special education eligibility process to one more focused on student capacities and strengths. These two rating scales, the Behavior & Emotional Rating Scale, Second Edition (BERS-2) and School Success Profile, are contained in the book's reference section (Bowen, Rose, & Bowen, 2005; Epstein & Sharma, 1998).

To change her special education assessment process, Jenny started with her own interviews. Using some material from SFBT, she reshaped her student interview and the family social development form to reflect more solution-focused and strength-based ideas (Gleason, 2007; Murphy, 1996). After completing the student interview and receiving the written social developmental study paperwork from each student's parents, she followed up with a phone call to the parents to confirm the information and explore what other information might be indicating that the student had begun to make changes in his/her academic or behavioral performance in the interval between the initial consent for the case study and the case study meeting (presession change). Finally, Jenny would ask the parents to complete a copy of the BERS-2 along with the student's classroom teacher, and used this BERS-2 data to help frame the student's difficulties in terms of strengths that he or she already exhibited and other areas that needed more work or were "emerging." (On the basis of the student's motivation and cognitive levels, she would also often ask the student to complete his or her own student version of the BERS-2, so that she had three sets of strength-oriented data on the student to triangulate and share.)

The next all-important step involved fashioning this new data and new perspectives into information that could be shared concisely at the student's special education eligibility meeting. This was no easy task, as each meeting was only scheduled for an hour and there was never any shortage of "problem talk" to get through regarding why the particular student wasn't behaving appropriately or learning at his or her grade level. Jenny elected to forego her usual read-through of her social history and instead use the BERS-2 data to help her focus on what she saw as the student's strengths and how those strengths might be enhanced to improve the referral problem specified for the case study evaluation.

SFBT Family Therapy

The literature on schools as "community schools" is growing, with attention being paid to helping whole families access services at schools after regular school hours (Anderson-Butcher, Iachini, & Wade-Mdivanian, 2007). Some of those services include after-school tutoring programs, ESL classes for parents, job training programs for teens, and mental health services (Hammond & Reimer, 2006). In the case study example that follows, one school social worker we worked with described a case where she saw a family of a student at her school for a six-session SFBT course of treatment.

> Carol (name changed for confidentiality)is a school social worker in the large suburban district of Forest Side, outside of Chicago. Fifty percent of the students in this district are on the free lunch program; 80% of the district's students are black, 15% are Latino, and 5% are white. Carol has worked in the district for 15 years, and over this period she has seen minimal improvement in the availability of family-based mental health services in the community, hampering her ability to make solid family therapy referrals for her neediest students. This past year, as part of her professional development goals, she decided to implement an intensive evening family therapy program utilizing SFBT ideas with the students on her caseload who appeared to have significant family struggles. She shared details of one of her cases with us.

The Case of Shantel and Her Lost Wisdom

Shantel Thomas (name changed for confidentiality) is an African American 7th grader who lives with her mother, step-father, and two younger brothers in Forest Side. Mrs. Thomas (now Mrs. Daniels after marrying Mr. Daniels 5 years ago and having her two children with him) has lived in Forest Side for all of Shantel's life. However, Shantel only recently moved back to Forest Side to live full-time with her mother and step-father. For the past 2 years, she had been living with her father and his girlfriend in Chicago, after having run away to her dad's house following a particularly bitter argument with her mother and step-father. Now she is back at Carol's school and is having a number of behavioral and academic adjustments, resulting in a number of discipline referrals. Carol observes that Shantel seems to be isolated from other girls in the school's lunchroom. What follows is the first family session where Carol uses scaling questions and the miracle question to mobilize the family around some new solutions for resolving the family's and Shantel's struggles.

Carol (C): Hello and welcome back to school! I hope you were able to get to my office with no hassle.

Mr. Daniels (Mr. D): Sure, the school secretary buzzed us in and pointed us up here.

Shantel (S): And I knew where it was, so I could show them!

C: That's great, you could be the tour guide for your parents. Did you show them anything else on your way up here, maybe like where your classroom is?

S: No, I just came here. They can find Ms. Frederick's room on their own time—ooh, I hate her!

Mrs. Daniels (Mrs. D): Shantel! Don't let me hear you talking about your teacher that way. It's only been a month since you started here and already you're talking badly about your teacher. (turning to Carol) See, this is her way. She doesn't given anybody a chance, just makes her mind up and well...

C: I'm wondering about that, too, Shantel. If you had to say on a scale of 1–5, with 1 being not at all comfortable here in your new school, and 5 saying that you were totally comfortable here, what would you say your rating is for being at our school?

S: (without hesitation) Oh, a 2 definitely. I mean, it's not like the school totally stinks, but it's nothing like my old school Washington.

C: So a 2 is what you would rate our school. What would you have said comfort scale was at Washington?

S: Definitely a 4, maybe even a 5. Yeah, I was real good there.

Mrs. D: You know, she's right about that. My ex-husband told me that Shantel never got any calls home while she was there, and she was even doing...what was that club you were in?

S: Wasn't a club, mama. I was in plays and I also did this after-school dance class too.

C: So not only did you rate your school time at Washington higher, you were doing after-school stuff as well?

S: Yeah, it was a great place.

C: What would be a way that you could do something at our school to make it feel more like you felt at Washington?

S: Hmm...I don't know.

C: Is there anything that you did at Washington that you think you could "bring" here?

S: I got it. I think I left something at Washington, with my old acting teacher.

C: Excuse me?

S: My acting teacher always talked about how we had to hold on to our wisdom while we were doing our parts. He said we all knew more about our characters than the audience did, and we had to hold on to that wisdom and pull it out when we were up there, to make us do a better job.

C: That's fascinating. He said you had wisdom, and how old are you?

S: You know how old I am. A lot younger than those two (pointing to mom, everybody laughs).

Mrs. D: Shantel, you are crazy, joking about all this and we're here to talk about your problems!

C: You know Mrs. Daniels, I think in some ways we are starting to talk about Shantel's problems here at our school. Can I tell you what I've seen happening at school, Shantel?

S: I guess.

C: I've talked to your teachers and they all told me—even Ms. Frederick!—that you are clearly one of the smartest kids in their class. You raise your hand a lot and have good things to contribute. They say that if you did their work, your first quarter grades would be all A's and B's.

S: Really? I thought they all hated me. They're always looking at me like I did something wrong.

Mr. D: What about the problems after school and in the lunchroom? I know it's only been a month, but my wife and I have gotten something like five calls from the school asking us to talk to Shantel and to come get her. Getting into fights, back-talking... This has got to stop.

S: They're always getting me into trouble! I told you, nobody likes me here (puts head down, seems ready to either leave the room or cry)!

C: Shantel, hold on a minute. What your step-dad is saying is true, right, about you getting into some trouble at our school?

S: Yeah, but what else can I do? These other girls are always acting like they own the school or something tellin' me where to sit, and oh man, don't get me started on those lunch supervisors... they're evil!

C: OK, I think I'm getting a better picture of why you rated our school a 2 for you. I want you to try something with me for a minute. Let's imagine that after we leave here today you go home with your parents, play with your little brothers, do your homework, and then go to sleep.

S: That's pretty much what I would do.

C: Great. But this is a different night of going to sleep, because while you are sleeping, a miracle happens to you and when you wake up and come back to school, everything that was a problem for you here is different, all the things that have been bothering you here are different somehow.

S: So... like all those mean girls and teachers are gone?

C: No, the miracle happens with everybody still at school, including you. What's different is that the problems are gone.

S: Hmm.

C: So, my question to you first, and then I'll ask your parents their answer, is, "what would you notice first was different?"

S: (thinks for a long time) I know: I'd have my wisdom again.

C: Tell me more about that.

S: All that wisdom I had at Washington, when I was acting and just being myself, I'd be able to get that back and use it to fight back here.

C: Can you give me an example of what you mean by using your wisdom to fight back?

S: Sure, with my wisdom, I would be able to see through the things the girls are saying to me, and just go off and make my own friends.

C: What else?

S: I'd be better at holding on to my comebacks when those evil lunch supervisors come around yelling at me, just look at them and smile or something and say, "yes" and then get away from them and go sit somewhere else.

C: Wait, with your wisdom you'd be able to do that? "See through" the other girls' comments and not get all mad back at the lunch supervisors?

S: Yeah, that's what I did at Washington. There were mean girls there, too. I just liked being there more, I guess.

C: So, let's take the miracle one step further and let me ask your parents the same question: what would be the first sign that the miracle had happened and things were better for Shantel at school?

Mrs. D: Shantel would be happy to go to school and wouldn't be so hard to live with at home (everybody laughs). I've got to be honest . . .

Mr. D: You got that right, Shantel, if you got some wisdom somewhere and you lost, you really need to go get it. I'll drive you to go pick it up (laughter again)!

Solution-Focused Needs Assessment

One of the gaps in the present SFBT literature involves the application of SFBT to organizational and community contexts. One of the most prominent examples of a solution-focused community organization is Garza School, which we dealt with in detail in Chapter 5. The notion of a solution-focused community organizer may sound far fetched, but in fact this is just what one of our colleagues became when she engaged in a series of solution-focused groups designed to help parents describe their goals for their children and the ways that they hoped that their neighborhood school could begin to address those needs.

Sarah (name changed for confidentiality) is a social worker employed by a local community mental health agency in an urban Midwestern city. The goal of her community outreach unit is to facilitate partnerships with local schools in inner-city communities to increase parent/school involvement and to also generate more use of the agency's family-based mental health and vocational services. Despite having conducted needs assessment and service outreach for two years as part of a grant-funded project, Sarah and her colleagues were finding that their parent clients, many of whom had multiple challenges related to living in poverty, still remained hard-to-reach and weren't using the services offered by the agency fully. In a similar vein, school officials reported frustration with parents who didn't participate in their child's education and seemed to only come to school when they "felt like it." These complaints are common to educators and practitioners trying to engage and involve parents coming from impoverished backgrounds (Comer, 2005).

As part of her start-up work in a new neighborhood school Tillman Elementary (name changed for confidentiality), Sarah decided to conduct her agency's needs assessment in a new way. She spent a few days visiting local neighborhood businesses, churches, and organizations and compiled a list of 15 community stakeholders who were parents of students at Tillman and who were interested in coming to a focus group to discuss the agency's outreach program. When she convened the group, she used the SFBT miracle question to help facilitate the discussion: "If a miracle happened overnight, and Tillman became a place that was more welcoming to parents, what would be different?" The answers didn't take long to surface: These parents said they spent most of their nonworking time taking care of young children, looking for employment, dealing with their own health issues at a range of different health care providers, or waiting at social welfare agencies to get their families services. Focus group members said that the first thing that would be different is that the school would have agencies offering them help at school, so that they could also be more present at school for the Tillman students.

Sarah and the agency team then brainstormed with the parent focus group on the range of services that would be ideal for them to have available at Tillman, and also on what format would best help them engage those services. The group agreed that having monthly "service fairs" on a particular day would be helpful for them to prioritize that day, and they also wondered whether this would help the school design a day or evening program for parents involving parent-teacher conferences and other activities. (Significantly, Sarah decided not to include school faculty and administration in this initial meeting; the thinking was that parents wouldn't be open in their comments, and school officials would be immediately put on the defensive. Subsequent meetings did involve members of the focus group and school administration.)

Sarah contacted several agencies that provided welfare and health care services to the community, and was surprised at how eagerly they embraced the idea. (They wanted to do innovative outreach for their services and thought that this was a fresh idea.) Within a month, the miracle question had helped create a little miracle at Tillman: a day-long "service fair" where parents could come and get health screenings, meet with local social welfare agencies, and also meet with their child's teachers. The service fairs have been held each month for the past year and are helping the administration at Tillman think about other ways in which they might reach out to parents whom they had previously thought of as indifferent to their children's education (Anderson-Butcher & Ashton, 2004).

SFBT Groups in Schools

Solutions to Anxiety

National survey data and health experts identify childhood anxiety as a growing and underresearched problem (American Academy of Child and Adolescent Psychiatrists, 2007). The literature on effective treatments for childhood anxiety emphasizes a combination of cognitive-behavioral therapy (CBT) and pharmacological intervention (Chorpita & Southam-Gerow, 2006), though most researchers in this area acknowledge the need for further study of the long-term impacts of antianxiety medication for children (Pollock & Kuo, 2004). One of the most promising areas of our recent practice has been our efforts to work with students identified with learning disabilities who also have a host of anxiety symptoms associated with their school performance.

Solution-Focused Brief Therapy in Schools

Box 6.1 contains a description of an 8-week solution-focused group intervention designed to help students coping with generalized anxiety disorder and those grappling with test anxiety. The group session was conducted with students at a suburban K-6 elementary school with a group of five 5th- and 6th-grade girls who either had been diagnosed with generalized anxiety disorder by outside mental health providers or had described significant anxiety to us in their social work weekly sessions as part of their individualized education plan (IEP) minutes. The group session was conducted during lunchtime for 8 consecutive weeks, and sessions took place as students ate lunch and socialized with each other.

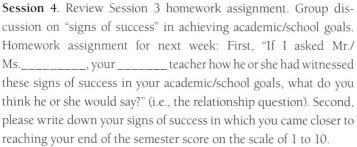

BOX 6.1 Eight-Week SFBT Group for Student Anxiety

Session 1. Introductions. Obtained informed consent for participation. Discussed group expectations. Discussed the goals of the group (i.e., to help students identify ways to manage their anxiety at home and school and cope with test anxiety).

Session 2. In-session assignment. "What academic/school goals do you have this semester?" and "What do you hope to achieve by participating in this group for the next 8 weeks?" Use of the miracle question.

Session 3. Use of the scaling question (i.e., "On a scale from 1 to 10, with 1 being your academic/school goals not achieved 10 meaning all your goals have been achieved, where would you rate yourself as a student today?") Homework assignment for next week: "Where would you like to be on the scale at the end of the semester?" and appraise the group on "What are the ways in which you will accomplish this increase?" (Goal and future oriented).

Session 4. Review Session 3 homework assignment. Group discussion on "signs of success" in achieving academic/school goals. Homework assignment for next week: First, "If I asked Mr./ Ms._____, your_____ teacher how he or she had witnessed these signs of success in your academic/school goals, what do you think he or she would say?" (i.e., the relationship question). Second, please write down your signs of success in which you came closer to reaching your end of the semester score on the scale of 1 to 10.

(continued)

Session 5. Review Session 4 homework assignment. Use the solution-focused brief therapy technique: EARS (i.e., elicit, amplify, reinforce, and start over). Use of the exception-finding question to amplify and reinforce present and future change.

Session 6. Revisit the scaling question. Homework assignment: A letter from the "older, wiser self" (Dolan, 1995). "Imagine that you have grown to be a healthy, wise old man or woman and you are looking back on this period of your life. What would this older and wiser man or woman suggest to you, which helped you get to where you are now in your academic/school goal(s)."

Session 7. Review Session 6 homework assignment. Discuss how the "new" self has emerged: Employ EARS.

Session 8. Review Session 7 homework assignment. Discuss setbacks as being normal. Pass out certificates of success.

Source: Adapted from Newsome, S. (2004). Solution-focused brief therapy (SFBT) group work with at-risk junior high school students: Enhancing the bottom-line. Research on Social Work Practice, 14(5), 336–343. Involving SFBT groups for middle school students.

A Solution-Focused Parent Group for GRGs

The number of school-aged children living with their grandparents has increased in the past 20 years, with the 2000 census data reporting that there are now over 4.5 million children living in grandparent-headed households (Davies, 2002). This population of new parents, who thought they had already finished being responsible for young children, is now assuming this new challenge, often under trying family, professional, and health circumstances (Fuller-Thomson & Minkler, 2000). To address the growing number of GRGs in our school community, we began to offer 8-week solution-focused parenting groups specifically designed for GRGs, and we offer a summary of the content of those group sessions below.

The group model discussed here is an 8-week GRG "Solution Group." The group would meet on school grounds, preferably at a time when most grandparents could attend. Although it is not absolutely essential that GRGs be grouped homogeneously, we suggest that novice SFBT practitioners try to implement a group program for this specific population first, to both learn the specific needs of GRGs and apply and test SFBT ideas with them.

The groups had the following topics for each week, with sample questions that we asked them for each weekly session, as well as some examples of SFBT group interactions drawn from our previous work in this area (Newsome & Kelly, 2004):

Week 1: Introductions and Orientation to SFBT GRG Ideas
What is the most important part of the problem that brought you here?

- What part of that problem would you like to work on first?
- What is/are your thought(s) about the problem you're having with your grandchild?
- What is the one thing you would like to learn as it relates to this problem from this group?

We found that as with any new group venture in a school, the first session is crucial. In this first session, we gave grandparents a chance to get to know us and the other members in the group, and the basic ideas behind the SFBT approach. We thought that it was important to normalize both their particular circumstances as GRGs and the model collaborative problem solving between group members. Because change is going to be the focus of the group, we're also eager to discuss in the first session how SFBT views the change process and to contrast that with other more deficit-based approaches. We've found that this approach allows us to immediately validate the GRGs for their experience and wisdom and to truly say that we believe that they are the experts on matters concerning their grandchildren, and we hope to draw on that expertise over the next eight sessions.

Week 2: Identifying Your Signature Strengths as a Grandparent and Applying Them to Your Mission as a GRG
- What are your signature strengths as a grandparent raising your grandchild? (Peterson & Seligman, 2004)
- How do you use your signature strengths as a grandparent raising a grandchild?

In our second session, we ask our GRG group members to complete a strengths questionnaire to help us frame future discussions of their strengths as grandparents. Peterson and Seligman (2004) offer a taxonomy of "signature strengths" and virtues to complement the categories of psychopathology described in the *DSM-IV* and an instrument called the Values in Action (VIA) questionnaire that can be taken by the GRGs online. In this second session, we begin to use the VIA, as well as written exercises and discussion, to help the GRGs analyze where and how they're using their strengths as a GRG.

Recently the benefits of using the VIA was found to be quite helpful with a GRG who had become the primary caregiver of her grandchildren. As such, the grandparent stated to the second author that she was hesitant to use her artistic and imaginative ability with her grandchildren (e.g., drawing, painting, building things, making games out of chores) because her daughter had raised them much more rigorously and harshly before she passed away. Through the use of the VIA and a discussion that helped the grandparent identify her signature strengths, the GRG recognized that she could still honor her daughter's memory while also applying her creativity with her grandchildren (Newsome & Kelly, 2004, p. 73).

Week 3: Starting Small—How Small Changes Can Become Big Solutions

- Since our group has started, what have you noticed that is already different about the main problem you came in with?
- What did you do to make those changes? What do you need to do to maintain those changes with your grandchild?

To help illustrate the use of the aforementioned questions, we want to share an example of a conversation that took place with a GRG during the SFBT group process:

Group Leader (GL): Welcome back, everyone. Tonight we want to start by discussing a time in the last three weeks that the problem or problems affecting your grandchild were not so overwhelming, and what you did as a grandparent to help ease or lessen those problems. Do we have anybody who can share with us tonight?

Ms. Valdez (MV): I will. I think my grandson is getting better at school.

GL: Really? Tell us how you know that.

MV: Well, my grandson was having trouble on the playground, getting in fights and all that, and they called me in.

GL: Who is "they" here that you're talking about?

MV: The school staff, they wanted him to stay off the playground.

GL: And all that was because they didn't think your grandson could handle being on the playground? Have you seen times when Juan could handle being on playgrounds with other kids?

MV: Yes, I told them "he'll find his way," we just have to pay attention. To prove it I went to school to watch him play on the playground. I saw that he was alone, and nobody was playing with him. I thought, "No wonder he's getting in trouble, he's trying to find any way possible to fit in." I told him to go see if he could play soccer with some of the kids on the playground—he loves to play—and he did!

GL: And you were able to show the school that some kids "can find their own way." You recalled how much your grandson loved playing soccer, and you helped him get in a game. And all that fighting stuff on the playground went away.

MV: Yep. All it took was a little attention. That's what these kids need, our attention.

The above practice vignette helps to highlight the use of how small changes can become big solutions. More importantly, the dialogue helps to illustrate how the group leader and Ms. Valdez uncovered an exception of how the problem (i.e., fighting on the playground) became less debilitating to her grandson (i.e., when he started playing soccer with other kids on the playground). Similarly, it helped to increase the hope and resilience of Ms. Valdez as a primary caregiver to her grandson as she faces the many challenges and opportunities presented to her throughout the academic school year (Newsome & Kelly, 2004, pp. 75–76).

(*Note:* The first 3 weeks are held consecutively; after that, GRG groups take place on a 2-week/monthly basis to emphasize the belief that GRGs can both support each other and act creatively and effectively on their own, without the aid of "experts" Selekman, 1993).

Week 4: What's Already Working? Identifying Exceptions to Presenting GRG Parenting Problems

- If you can imagine our final meeting and being able to rate your problem as being low, what will have changed between then and now? What is the first thing you might do as a grandparent raising a grandchild to make this change happen?
- On a scale from 1 to 10 (with 1 being not coping at all with your new role and 10 being coping very well with your new role), how well would you say you are coping? What would be different in your life if you went from a 6 to a 7 or from a 7 to an 8?

To help illustrate the use of the scaling question as a way to find exceptions, we are excerpting a portion of a conversation we had with a GRG during a group session several years ago:

Group Leader (GL): O.K., tonight I would like you to think of something you've been working on changing with your grandchild. It can be something you've been working on at home or at school. I want you to rate how well you think your grandchild has been doing on a scale from 1 to 10, with 1 being very poor and 10 being very excellent. Would anyone like to start us off?

Ms. Wilson (MW): My granddaughter, she has been fighting with her older brother too much, especially when it's time for them to get down to their schoolwork.

GL: How would you rate her level of fighting with her brother in the last few weeks on a scale of 1 to 10, with 1 being very excessive and 10 being not excessive at all?

MW: You know I was thinking before you asked me. Early on, I would have said it was very excessive, I would have given her a 1, but lately I'd say she's been making an effort. I think I would rate her at a 5, maybe a 6.

GL: And that 5 or 6 is better than it was before?

MW: Oh yes! She was down around a 1 for too, too long.

GL: What do you think brought her up from a 1 to 5?

MW: I've been just telling her to go to another room, and leaving it at that. I gave up yelling and cussing back at her—it didn't work. Besides, doing this gives her nobody to talk to and soon after she shapes up and starts saying "grandma, I'll be good, I promise."

GL: That's great. So, you're doing something different helps her decide to behave differently. What do you think needs to happen for your granddaughter to get to a 7 or 8?

MW: That would be amazing to see her at a 7 or 8. I think if she figures out that I'm serious about not letting her mess with her brother, she'll calm down. I can see her getting to that 7 or 8 someday.

In this practice vignette, the group leader used the scaling question with Ms. Wilson as a way to recognize the proactive change that has occurred over the last few weeks. More than that, however, the scaling question helped to open up a discussion of the progress and growth made by her grandchild and Ms. Wilson. By using the scaling question, the group leader was also able to tap into Ms. Wilson's practical wisdom in addressing a very common issue between two siblings (Newsome & Kelly, 2004, pp. 77–78).

Week 5: The "Doing Something Different Day:" Using SFBT Interventions in Daily Life With Your Grandchildren

Week 6: Maintaining Change: Ways to Keep Change Going as a GRG

- What are two things you could do differently this week as a grandparent raising a grandchild as it relates to your problem?
- What are a few impacts you might imagine happening as a result of "doing something differently?"

Week 7: GRG Wisdom Night—A Panel of Elders Share Their Life's Lessons

(For this session, we invite other GRG "elders" in the school community to share their wisdom in a panel discussion.)

- Looking back at your experience in this group at week one, what is different about your "parenting role?"
- Who in your life views you as a person who has wisdom to share?

Week 8: Change Party: A Celebration of the Changes Already Made With the Help of SFBT and Those Changes to Come

- What is new and powerful about you as a grandparent raising a grandchild? How can you maintain this new part of you as a grandparent raising a grandchild?
- What have you learned about your grandchild's strengths and capacity to change?
- What is the most important lesson you learned in this group and who taught you this lesson?

SFBT Technique: A Celebration of Change

In keeping with the SFBT philosophy, we choose to deal with group endings and termination issues by focusing on the positive aspects of the group. As a result, we have a "change party." In using the change party technique, each GRG brings his/her grandchild to the group and shares one thing that has changed in the past three to four months as well as one strength that they most admire about each of their grandchildren. (Each of the GRGs will have done a signature strength VIA with each of his/her grandchildren at this point, to have that instrument to draw on.)

While the majority of this final group is spent socializing and having fun, we do encourage the GRGs to consider forming some kind of informal network with us or other group members to help build on the positive solutions and relationships that the group helped to foster (Newsome & Kelly, 2004, p. 80).

The Future

This is just a sampling of what a solution-focused school professional could do with SFBT ideas. What are your ideas now, after reading this chapter? Can you think of a place or population in your school community that might benefit from some solution-focused interventions? Starting small is a good idea; find a classroom or group of students and get started. After all, as we learned in Chapter 2, solution-focused practice teaches us that small changes can lead to big ones. Feel free to take any of these ideas and implement them in your school context by either consulting the available research on the intervention or contacting one of us at our e-mail at the end of this chapter. Start small, start now; have fun with solution-focused work in your school!

7

■■■

SFBT's Next 25 Years: Possibilities and Challenges Ahead for SFBT in Schools

This chapter will involve a question-and-answer format, where we ask leading solution-focused brief therapy (SFBT) practitioners and researchers about their views on SFBT in schools and the challenges they see ahead to making SFBT more accepted and utilized in education.

1. Do you view SFBT as a distinct therapy technique or model? Does SFBT's distinctiveness (or lack thereof) really matter, and if so, how?

Linda Metcalf, PhD, LPC, LMFT, author of *Counseling Toward Solutions*, Assistant Professor, Texas Woman's University: SFBT has emerged from MRI like other models so I would hesitate to call it distinct. I do not see it as a technique, more, a way of thinking about clients. I don't think its being distinctive matters at all. In fact, most people I know that use SFBT like the fact that it is so flexible in its use and application. I simply like it because it is respectful and helpful.

Steve Hunter, LCSW, SFBT, private practice therapist and Brief Family Therapy Center Trainee, in the 1980s with Berg and de Shazer: I view it as both (a therapy technique and a model). It is a philosophy on change and how people change. This model and philosophy was given to us by our clients and what they find useful. The school social worker is not the expert on the client's life. Although contrary to medical models, SFBT is a way of thinking and constructing solutions. It is essentially a set of beliefs about change.

Victoria Baldwin, Principal of Garza School, Austin, Texas: It is absolutely distinct for educators. It does not come natural or just roll off the tongue. It had to be taught, valued, and we have to go back and relearn it again. We have to relearn it continuously because we are conditioned to be punitive. We are bombarded by an accusing approach. Training is needed and it definitely takes more than one time to sustain a solution-focused approach. It is a philosophy that has to be embraced and it has to get into the culture of the school. I still have a tendency to relapse back and you have to go back to it. I have learned from solution building that it works to give voice, and respect to students and they will respond in kind. So, I go back to it. The results are astonishing—quiet, peaceful, and spiritual. The kids become protective of that kind of environment. They act to protect the school. We are almost 10 years old and protection of the school has been a prevalent theme.

John Murphy, PhD, Professor of Psychology and Counseling, University of Central Arkansas, co-author with Barry Duncan of *Brief Intervention for School Problems, Second Edition: Outcome-Informed Strategies (Guilford School Practitioner Series):* Although SFBT promotes several distinct values and assumptions about people and therapy, I prefer not to see it as yet another in the long line of therapy models. Over 250 so-called models have been identified in the literature, none of which have proven universally superior to any others in overall effectiveness. Though it is impossible to completely separate model and technique factors from other ingredients of effective therapy—client participation, client resources, therapeutic alliance, and hope—research has consistently indicated that effective outcomes result more from these nonspecific ingredients than from the specific ingredients of a particular model (e.g., miracle question, homework assignments, and so forth). So, I would say that the effectiveness of SFBT and any other approach or technique lies in its usefulness in (1) engaging the client's participation and hope, and (2) accommodating the client's values, goals, opinions, strengths, feedback, and other resources. The extent to which these nonspecific ingredients are part of the therapy process is up to the school social worker, not the model. Every school social worker implements his or her approach differently. Some are more attuned to the client's goals and contributions, and will be more effective as a result, regardless of how they label themselves or their model.

For the above reasons, I would prefer not to place SFBT into the ever-growing conga line of therapy models. This is more than a semantic issue. The more popular a therapy approach becomes, the more likely it is to gain the reified status as a "model." One unfortunate result of this is that practitioners may become so focused on implementing the model that they lose sight of the client's uniqueness and the therapeutic relationship. Therapy works best when we adapt our methods to clients instead of squeezing them into our preferred models and techniques. As SFBT continues to evolve and gain popularity among practitioners, it will become even more important to sustain a client-driven perspective that prioritizes the goals, resources, and perceptions of clients over the "model" and techniques. Research makes it clear that techniques are the means to therapeutic ends, not the ends in themselves. For example, the miracle question is a means to developing client-directed goals and positive expectancy. If it is not working, then it is best to simply move on and try something else. This is not meant to downplay the usefulness of techniques. Everything we do with clients can be considered techniques, including questions, suggestions, homework assignments, and so forth. My comments are aimed at keeping techniques in their proper perspective in relation to all-important client factors and other ingredients of effective therapy.

Sean Newsome, PhD, MSW, Assistant Professor and Director of the BSW Program, Miami University, author of five articles on school social work SFBT practice: As with many supportive, therapeutic models, SFBT does appear to be influenced by a variety of theories. In particular, SFBT appears to include elements of cognitive, behavioral, cognitive-behaviorism, and the strengths perspective. However, unlike many of the aforementioned theories, SFBT is a collaborative shift for the practitioner and the client(s) from one of pathology and problems to that of solutions. In fact, many of the techniques utilized by SFBT practitioners emphasize a collaborative movement in which the practitioner is compelled to take a more optimistic view of his or her client(s).

Robin Bluestone-Miller, LCSW, School Social Worker and WOWW trainer at Loyola's Family and Schools Partnership Program (FSPP): SFBT is a distinct model because it relies on a specific set of assumptions and communication techniques that are not specific to other models. Even though, it is strength based and narrative techniques can be incorporated into SFBT, but it is so much more than that. It has been compared to cognitive behavior therapy, but it is a more collaborative therapy where clients set their own goals and how they judge efficacy. Relationships are also very important and there is the inherent assumption that change can and will happen.

2. What evidence would you recommend school-based practitioners to use if they wanted to demonstrate the promise of SFBT's effectiveness in schools to school administrators?

Bluestone-Miller: The research by Cynthia Franklin on the Garza Independence High School demonstrates that solution-focused techniques can be adapted to a school setting. The entire staff was trained to use solution-based communications in dealing with students, not only the counseling staff, which helped everyone remain strength based and positive with this high-risk population. The graduation rate was a powerful outcome.

I have been involved with a pilot research program with Loyola University and Chicago Public Schools, called WOWW program: A solution-focused classroom intervention. Our initial results show that teachers see an improvement with their own classroom management skills. They also have a more positive perception that students are better behaved and more respectful after a 10-week WOWW program in their school. We already know that if the teachers have a more positive outlook on their students, they will treat them better and have higher expectations for them. Additionally, many students gained in self-awareness and felt empowered to work on changing their classroom behaviors. We believe that these changes will lead to more school success like improved grades, attendance, and positive behavior patterns. We are continuing to evaluate these outcomes.

Baldwin: Show discipline statistics to the board and make a proposal. There are very few districts that do not have a problem with angry and disenfranchised youth regardless of socioeconomic status.

Disruptive behavior interferes with the main mission of the school. A school that is out of control will sacrifice the student's achievement and success, and the board and administrators will be receptive to improvements in discipline because the parents will lose confidence in schools that are not safe. It is important to look at the research on solution focused and show the board. Help the board understand that it is a philosophy that has to be adopted instead of just a few pat methods.

Newsome: The importance of presenting evidence-based practice to school stakeholders cannot be overstated. As such, I feel it is vitally important that school-based practitioners "arm" themselves with research that can articulate and demonstrate the potential effectiveness of SFBT. This includes both conceptual and applied research studies that speak to the potential use of SFBT with at-risk school populations as well as those studies that have tested the effectiveness and utility of SFBT with at-risk school populations. As such, it has been my experience that school administrators, teachers and parents want to see supportive material that shows the various techniques utilized by SFBT practitioners as well as the possible impact of SFBT on behavior, school attendance and GPA. Presenting the possibilities and potential impact of SFBT addresses the current educational reform movements that highlight the importance of improving student behavior and performance while also addressing a school's need to recognize cost-effective interventions in their school district. Studies that can be shared with school stakeholders that report the effectiveness and utility of SFBT are vital during a period of time in which K-12 educators emphasize the bottom-line, hard-data and accountability.

Metcalf: The selection and framing of a "demonstration strategy" will depend partly on what is most important to the particular administrator. For example, emphasizing that SFBT promotes client "buy-in" may be effective with an administrator who is very litigation conscious, in that the client's buy-in greatly reduces the probability of lawsuits resulting from gross misunderstandings between clients and practitioners. Likewise, an administrator who wants to promote more parent involvement may respond positively to the notion that SFBT seeks out and honors input from parents as well as others involved with students who are referred for services. Regardless of these unique features related to local schools and administrators, student-based outcome data "should" be the best evidence for demonstrating the usefulness of SFBT or any other school service. These data can be compiled across the school year for individual practitioners or entire service departments (e.g., across the entire social work or counseling department).

3. Are there any "pre-" steps to implement in a school or academic team before exposing them to SFBT ideas that might make the adoption of SFBT ideas go more smoothly?

Baldwin: You have to develop a rationale that works with business on a daily basis. The principal should use the school's data on suspension, expulsion and student achievement. If a caustic culture exists the school might be open to a philosophy like solution focused that provides a more humane environment. Help them understand that it is one approach to learn that can help. Not that teachers know how but they want to do it. Solution focused can help them get from good to great.

It is important to show its advantages to the school. Questions to ask: Are you satisfied in the way your school operates in behavior and all aspects of achievement? Are you sitting back and knowing your school can do better? Confronting questions is important. If you are going to change you have to be ready to do something different. Show solution focused as a way of communication and improvement of relationships. It can even help them with their personal relationships with their families and friends.

Help schools deal with the fear that if you let your guard down something bad is going to happen. Show them the opposite is true. Fear and control do not work! So, it is time to change their ideas. Teachers want to learn and my teachers now point out to me that when I don't use solution-focused. Most parents also want their children to succeed and by using solution-focused we can do better with parents. My teachers ask for more training. We are still learning. You have to bring in coaches, and small reminders to stay on track. Even taping instructions to your desk.

Newsome: As with any potential model being used in school settings, it is paramount that schools and/or academic teams be on board. Educating school administrators, teachers and staff to the inherent differences of SFBT to that of traditional models as well as getting the district behind the implementation of SFBT is crucial. This means conducting workshops; using various SFBT video for instruction; role playing the various techniques utilized in the model and articulating how the SFBT model fits with the strengths-based initiatives expected of school practitioners in both general and special education. Some additional "pre" steps to implementation include pointing out the "briefness" of the model and how the techniques of SFBT offer options in being able to respond and act quickly to the needs of students and children at-risk. Even more important is that individuals recognize that SFBT is not limited to supportive, therapeutic settings. To the point, an essential "pre" step to implementation is for school or academic teams to recognize the SFBT model as a way of life. Specifically, a "pre" step for the adoption of SFBT is to articulate how the model and its core components (i.e., collaboration, focus on strengths not deficits, focus on present and future behaviors, identifies solutions rather that amplifying problems and importance of goal setting) might fit or be imbedded in a school's mission and their overall goals for the school district. From this standpoint, school administrators and school personnel may "share" the view of ownership once the implementation of SFBT begins.

Metcalf: I think the "proof is in the pudding," and when using any new model or idea in schools, it is the "buy-in" that matters to the principal and staff. When I began my one year job as a high school counselor, with a SFBT approach, staff was not interested in what model I used, they were interested in results. I soon learned to make each staff member and parent and student my school client.

There is a lot of talk about evidence-based practice and while solution-focused therapy has fewer studies than some, it is acknowledged more by managed health care and insurance companies for its effectiveness. To summarize, just do the model and school staff will come.

Bluestone-Miller: Belief in the solution-based assumptions are the heart and soul of being able to do training and counseling in SFBT. Believing that change is inevitable and that no behavior happens all of the time, and there are always exceptions to the problem; help those who practice this model, see hope for a future without the problem. It is imperative for a school or team to understand and BELIEVE these assumptions in order to successfully use the model.

4. What are some of the most important things to know when doing SFBT techniques in groups with students?

Bluestone-Miller: It helps to take a "Colombo approach" and be very curious. Most students are surprised when you say things like, "You must have a very good reason for doing problematic behaviors like, skipping school or taking drugs." Students, parents and educators react in a very positive and encouraging manner when someone acknowledges their strengths and compliments them for something that they are doing well. These parents have become used to feeling criticized in school meetings and often react defensively. A SFBT approach is collaborative and empowering for the client.

Newsome: Groups allow for the development of mutual aid and support among those presenting similar circumstances. Beyond the most recent and positive developments of SFBT in school settings, the SFBT group model helps to create new meanings, perceptions and solutions with group participants. Group practitioners using SFBT in school settings should look to emphasize what individual members are already doing well, or have the potential to do well, as a way to facilitate goal achievement among all group members. Similarly, SFBT practitioners should seek to utilize the strengths presented by its members while also shifting beliefs and unproductive interactions. To achieve such proactive change, SFBT practitioners in schools should utilize the resources and strengths presented by the group and each student; recognize that positive change for the group and each student is inevitable; use the past only for context; practice from a present and future orientation; be cooperative and collaborative; identify solutions rather than magnifying problems for individuals and the group; discuss exceptions to problems as building blocks to solutions, and lastly, construct goals for each individual and the group. Despite these considerations for SFBT group practice in school settings, one must also be willing to modify any "working" group.

As such, SFBT group practice should reflect the desires and needs of its clientele and allow maximum input concerning the changes they want to build on in the group. SFBT group practice, therefore, should strive to fashion an environment where its group members can proceed to co-create their experiences in the group setting.

5. One of the main beliefs in SFBT is that clients are able to make good decisions and be in charge of finding their own solutions. Are there ever clients (clients with severe mental illness, adolescents engaging in high-risk behaviors, substance abusing clients) for whom SFBT is not appropriate? If so, what other techniques would you recommend employing with those clients?

Hunter: Safety for the student and others is always paramount. SFBT is not operating from a social control paradigm. Therefore, students who are at great risk due to a variety of factors need stabilizers. That may take several different forms. That said, I have dealt with clients who have psychosis, chemical dependency, and acting out with SFBT. Schools and school-based practitioners must find a balance to preserve client safety and still collaborate with local mental health agencies to incorporate SFBT principles.

Metcalf: I think there will always be school clients that need us to be school social workers first and take care of them and model followers, second. However, the thinking and the manner in which I approach that challenging client will always be solution focused in that I will:

1. Always let the client tell me what we can do during the session that will be helpful in a crisis.
2. Always be respectful in their endeavor, whether it is cutting, hurting others, using drugs, drinking, etc. I do and will always ask "how is this behavior helpful to you?" so that my client knows I am listening.

I think it is important (and I tell my students this) that no matter what model we use to work with clients, that it is a model that works for us, personally. Therefore, there would not be other techniques I would use. I would simply follow my client's lead. Of course, if the client is actively suicidal, I will ethically make arrangements for the client to be taken care of but I will also try to connect that action with an exception that I try to learn about the client. For example, if the client talks to me and tells me things that are uncomfortable, that is an exception and I will compliment him on that.

Murphy: I believe that giving clients the invitation and opportunity to have a voice in decisions affecting their lives is appropriate with all clients in all circumstances. The existence of a diagnostic label or high-risk circumstance should never disqualify or discredit the person's voice when it comes to decisions affecting them—unless (1) they are literally disabled from indicating their input (e.g., unable to communicate), or (2) they knowingly and willingly choose for someone else to make such decisions or offer input. For various reasons, clients may request our opinions or the opinions and decisions of other trusted people in their lives. This is very different than removing that choice from people based solely on our judgment of "what is best for them" or that "they are too 'disturbed' to think for themselves." Besides the fact that I would not want or allow this to happen to me against my will or without my consent (an ethical yardstick that I've found helpful in many situations), we are not in a position to accurately make this judgment for someone else. Do we ever really know exactly how "disturbed" someone is? Of course we don't, but even if we did, what level or degree of "disturbance" warrants exclusion from the decision-making process? I am not denying the existence of obviously debilitating circumstances and problems that compromise people's ability to make good decisions and judgments (e.g., shock, acute trauma, altered states of consciousness, and so forth). Beyond these obvious circumstances, however, I believe we should do whatever we can to ensure people the dignity and respect to participate in their recovery and treatment to the extent that they choose. In addition to the issues of respect and ethics, client participation is the most potent ingredient in successful therapeutic change.

Before putting the disturbance issue to rest, we should note that diagnosis has never lived up to its original billing. Although it continues to serve logistical functions such as meeting state requirements or receiving third-party payments, none of this is related to client outcomes. Diagnosis of psychological and behavioral problems is highly unreliable and invalid, especially with children and adolescents.

Diagnosis fails to reliably distinguish between the so-called pathological states themselves, or between these disorders and normal development variations or problems of living. Given these validity and reliability problems, it should come as no surprise that diagnosis has also fallen short on its promise to predict outcomes and select interventions. Several studies have indicated that "severity of the problem" is a much weaker predictor of outcome compared to client involvement, therapeutic relationship, and other such factors. Thus, to exclude young people from having a voice in their treatment based on a diagnostic label—regardless of how "severe" the label sounds or is purported to be—is based on legend versus facts.

Since this is a book about schools, I also want to address this issue as it pertains to students of all ages. I believe that students' voices and goals have been sadly underutilized. As the undisputed primary clients of school intervention, students are in an ideal position to contribute to the goals, tasks, and evaluation of intervention services.

6. Are there any additional comments or ideas you would like to share with our readers about what you think are key practice and research issues for the next decade of SFBT in schools?

Bluestone-Miller: Parent education and training programs using S-F techniques. It would be interesting to develop a solution-focused SDS for use in schools.

I would hope that another school model like Garza can be duplicated in the United States. There have been a few solution-focused special education schools operating in Europe since 1990s, but it would be impressive to develop a school with an inclusion model.

Hunter: There is a need for small research projects with SFBT that are well-done and published that deal with a variety of school contexts—urban, suburban, and rural. Additionally, it would be helpful for researchers and practitioners to collaborate on a multischool venture, incorporating interventions that involve SFBT group counseling, pupil personnel meetings, and teacher consultation.

Metcalf: I think today's school counselors are literally challenged each day. When I do workshops, I often ask about what percentage of their students respond to typical, traditional models such as CBT. I get the same everywhere . . . about 89%. But the 20% of the students that don't care and need someone to care, disrupt class and do harm to themselves. These are the students that I encourage school counselors to begin using the approach with. As a former school counselor on all levels who has used SFBT with many school clients, I see it as a novel and helpful way to begin changing the school climate, which will bring longer lasting change to students.

Newsome: Continued work is needed on the potential effectiveness of SFBT in school settings with at-risk and diverse populations on academic and behavioral indicators. Future research designs that look to test the effectiveness of SFBT should incorporate statistical analyses that look at maintenance and change over time when working with at-risk and diverse populations. Specifically, future research looking at the treatment effectiveness of SFBT must consider and determine the extent to which change in academic and behavioral areas are maintained for one school year to the next as well as the impact of SFBT on students transitioning from one school to another school or from primary education to secondary education. This is of special importance, given the current federal, state and local focus on "achievement" in our school systems.

Murphy: More research is always helpful in figuring out what is most helpful about what we're doing with clients. At this stage, several studies have demonstrated positive effects of SFBT for a variety of complaints. However, we haven't been able to reliably tease out the most potent or active ingredients of SFBT from the "whole package" in these situations. This is a huge empirical challenge for any approach, but a worthwhile question in the face of growing empirical evidence regarding the impact of nonspecific factors such as client involvement, relationship, hope, and so forth. From where I am standing at the moment, I think the best way to pursue this is to develop and implement practical ways to obtain client feedback throughout and following the therapy process. This will enable clients to continue to teach us what works and what doesn't, one client at a time, and may eventually lead to some generalizations that are applicable to most clients and circumstances—or not. Either way, it seems a worthwhile effort. I think we need to hold techniques lightly and be willing to try something else when they aren't working for the person sitting in front of us. Nothing works all the time with every client, and we need to make sure to keep it solution focused versus solution forced.

The insights and wisdom from these SFBT pioneers, researchers, and practitioners show both the depth and breadth of SFBT as it enters its next 25 years. Garza's Principal Victoria Baldwin calls the SFBT approach something that can transform the culture of an entire school to the point where the "quiet, peaceful, and spiritual" quality of the school becomes something that students strive to maintain and preserve. Our book's summary of SFBT research to date shows that SFBT can "compete" with more well-known treatments like CBT as a school-based intervention. SFBT has indeed come a long way from its beginnings in Milwaukee in the 1980s.

But as Linda Metcalf and others argue, maybe winning a competition for best therapy approach isn't really the goal of SFBT, and shouldn't be. Because the portable and strength-based nature of SFBT allows it to be combined with many diverse approaches to working in schools, SFBT allows practitioners to sidestep the field's misguided preoccupation with DSM-based diagnosis and to instead focus on solving student problems and demonstrating that SFBT is a practical, easy-to-use approach.

John Murphy rightly points out that DSM diagnoses have always had reliability and validity problems, and only a tenuous connection to actual client treatment outcomes. SFBT, by seeking to give clients a voice in their own treatment, is more than just a nicer or more positive way to work with students. It is one (effective) way for us to help our students and our schools flourish in an era that is heavily dominated by the medical model in mental health and special education labels in education.

Postscript

By Cynthia Franklin, Stiernberg/Spencer Family Professor in Mental Health, University of Texas-Austin

As this book suggests, over the past 12 years, SFBT has been growing in schools and has now reached its adolescence. Like most adolescents, SFBT is mature enough to drive but still has a lot of growing to do before its full potential can be realized. Authors across disciplines (e.g., social work, counseling, and psychology) have written about the potential of SFBT for school settings and researchers have also investigated its potential with promising findings. This book has offered a 360-degree view, discussing both practice applications and the research studies that support the use of SFBT in schools. School social workers are using SFBT in diverse ways from clinical approaches with students and families to programmatic approaches designed to impact teachers, classrooms, and even entire schools. This book has also illustrated the flexibility and transportability of SFBT by showing how social workers can train teachers and administrators to use SFBT and further use its strengths-based philosophy to transform the school climate and learning environment of a school.

My own journey using and researching SFBT started about 15 years ago when Peter DeJong introduced me to Insoo Kim Berg and Steve de Shazer, the codevelopers of the SFBT model. At that time, I was working with a youth agency that used SFBT and was conducting some single-case experiments on outcomes. I was also experimenting with the use of SFBT in my private practice. I was very eager to apply SFBT in a school setting because I believed it would be an excellent approach for school social workers and other practitioners to use. I later saw the potential for school social workers to train teachers and school staff in SFBT as a transdisciplinary approach to enable them to engage and work more effectively with students at-risk for dropping out of school.

Insoo Kim Berg was very encouraging toward my work and offered me more training in SFBT, as well as training support for my research team. Her efforts did much to increase the treatment fidelity of my research studies. For example, the first research study that I did in a school in 1996–1997 was strengthened by the fact that Insoo Kim Berg and Steve de Shazer trained all the staff in an intensive training in Milwaukee. During this time, Insoo and I also discussed the advantages of gathering a network of researchers around the SFBT model to further develop its empirical base. Peter DeJong and I worked together to have Insoo placed on the program of the Council on Social Work Education (CSWE) to present a workshop and to discuss the need for more research with interested faculty.

From that point on I supported the research development of the SFBT model and was very fortunate to enjoy a friendship and partnership with Insoo Kim Berg, who shared my vision to advance practice and research on SFBT in the schools. Insoo became a mentor to my research at Garza High School and she also worked with Lee Schilts to develop the WOWW program in Ft. Lauderdale, Florida. Insoo was an excellent mentor and I admired her sense of humor and clinical skills very much. I saw in her the embodiment

Solution-Focused Brief Therapy in Schools

of the values of social work practice to treat each person with dignity and worth and to help others to help themselves be the best that they can be. She truly believed that all people could change and that they had in them the abilities to build their own solutions. She shared characteristics with other great social work practitioners (e.g., Helen Harris Perlman; Bill Reid; Dennis Saleeby)—the importance of focusing on human capacities and strengths in the change process. Insoo was also a great networker and she traveled the world providing training workshops on SFBT, which made it possible for her to connect practitioners and researchers across continents. For this reason, people from around the world also came to hear of Garza High School on the basis of the experiences she shared. This resulted in Garza High School receiving many visitors from United States, Europe, and Japan so that educators could study the solution-focused school. Garza faculty, staff, and even students have also been invited from around the world (e.g., Romania, Ireland, and Japan) to discuss the educational practices of Garza.

Recently, a graduate from Garza High School named Carl visited Japan at the invitation of a Japanese therapist, Yuichi Takenouchi. Carl was featured in a training video on working with suicidal youth, "I'm Glad to Be Alive," which Insoo and I filmed at Garza High School. In the video, Carl mentioned his dream of going to Japan and also the fact that he was studying the Japanese language in school. This video landed in the hands of Yuichi Takenouchi and his practice group in Japan (Solution Land, http:// www.solution-land.com/eng/index_eng.html), and this group felt in their heart that they wanted to make Carl's dream come true and also wanted to interview him about his experiences attending Garza High School.

Interestingly, during his visit, Carl said he saw a strange bright light like a fire in the sky. Yuichi Takenouchi told him that it was a fire ball. At that moment, Carl was also reminded of Insoo, and even though she was not present, he told me, he could still feel that she was with him. Insoo obviously had a great impact on Carl's life. Sadly, this book was written on the heels of Insoo Kim Berg's death, but I hope that it will continue to make her presence felt by telling our readers SFBT school stories, as these ideas continue to move across the continents. I believe that SFBT is like that bright light that Carl saw and even though the progenitors of the approach are no longer present, SFBT's influence will still be felt in our field.

The future for SFBT is very bright with many world-wide contributors to its development. This current book advances the practices of SFBT by providing a state-of-the-art practice manual and research guide for those who wish to apply SFBT in schools. I believe the next steps that will hasten SFBT out of its adolescence to become a mature practice approach are for practitioners and researchers to work together to provide well-designed research studies. It is also time to take advantage of the best features of the SFBT model and those are its transportability, flexibility, and ecumenical attributes. No model stays the same or stands alone and continues to do what is best for clients. Future applications and studies on SFBT in schools may involve integrative approaches that use SFBT in combination with other approaches (e.g., CBT and Motivational Interviewing) to design the most effective intervention programs that are possible.

References

Aloise-Young, P. A., & Chavez, E. L. (2002). Not all school dropouts are the same: Ethnic differences in the relation between reason for leaving school and adolescent substance use. *Psychology in Schools, 39*(5), 539–547.

Altshuler, S. J., & Kopels, S. (2003). Advocating in schools for children with disabilities: What's new with IDEA? *Social Work, 48*(3), 320–329.

American Academy of Child and Adolescent Psychiatrists. (2007). Facts on anxiety. Retrieved August 3, 2007, from http://www.aacap.org/cs/root/developmentor/advances_in_child_and_adolescent_anxiety_disorder_research

Anderson-Butcher, D., & Ashton, D. (2004). Innovative models of collaboration to serve children, youth, families, and communities. *Children & Schools, 26*(1), 39–53.

Anderson-Butcher, D., Iachini, A., & Wade-Mdivanian, R. (2007). *School linkage protocol technical assistance guide: Expanded school improvement through the enhancement of the learning support continuum.* Columbus, OH: College of Social Work, Ohio State University.

APA Presidential Task Force on Evidence-Based Practice (2006). Evidence-based practice in psychology. *American Psychologist, 61*, 271–285.

Babcock, J. C., Green, C. E., & Robie, C. (2004). Does batterers' treatment work? A meta-analytic review of domestic violence treatment. *Clinical Psychology Review, 23*, 1023–1053.

Baumeister, R. F., Campbell, J. D., Krueger, J. I., & Vohs, K. D. (2003). Does self-esteem cause better performance, interpersonal success, happiness, or healthier lifestyles? *Psychological Science in the Public Interest, 4*(1), 1–44.

Berg, I., & Dolan, Y. (2001). *Tales of solutions: A collection of hope-inspiring stories.* New York: W. W. Norton.

Berg, I., & Shilts, L. (2005). *Classroom solutions: WOWW coaching.* Milwaukee, WI: BFTC Press.

Berg, I., & Shilts, L. (2005). *Classroom solutions: WOWW approach.* Milwaukee, WI, BFTC Press.

Berg, I. K. (1994). *Family-based services.* New York: W. W. Norton.

Bowen, G., Rose, R. A., & Bowen, N. K. (2005). *The reliability and validity of the school success profile.* Philadelphia: Xlibris Press.

Cade, B., & O'Hanlon, W. H. (1993). *A brief guide to brief therapy.* New York: W. W. Norton.

Chambless, D. L. (2002). Beware the Dodo bird: The dangers of overgeneralization. *Clinical Psychology: Science and Practice, 9,* 13–19.

Chambless, D. L., & Ollendick, T. H. (2001). Empirically supported psychological interventions: Controversies and Evidence. *Annual Review of Psychology, 52,* 685–716.

Chorpita, B. F., & Southam-Gerow, M. (2006). Fears and anxieties. In E. J. Mash & R. A. Barkley (Eds.), *Treatment of child disorders* (3rd ed., pp. 271–335). New York: Guilford.

Cockburn, J. T., Thomas, F. N., & Cockburn, O. J. (1997). Solution-focused therapy and psychosocial adjustment to orthopedic rehabilitation in a work hardening program. *Journal of Occupational Rehabilitation, 7,* 97–106.

Comer, J. P. (2005). The rewards of parent participation. *Educational Leadership, 62*(6), 38–42.

Constable, R. (2006). *21st century school social work*: Plenary address at the Family and Schools Partnership Program, July 2006.

Corcoran, J. (2006). A comparison group study of solution-focused therapy versus "treatment-as-usual" for behavior problems in children. *Journal of Social Service Research, 33*(1), 69–81.

Corcoran, J., Miller, P., & Bultman, L. (1997). Effectiveness of prevention programs for adolescent pregnancy: A meta analysis. *Journal of Marriage and the Family, 59,* 551–567.

Corcoran, J., & Stephenson, M. (2000). The effectiveness of solution-focused therapy with child behavior problems: A preliminary study. *Families in Society, 81*(5), 468–474.

Council on Social Work Education. (2004). Preamble. Retrieved March 6, 2004, from http://www.cswe.org/

Cushman, P. (1995). *Constructing the self, constructing America: A cultural history of psychotherapy.* Reading, MA: Addison-Wesley.

Davies, C. (2002). The Grandparent Study 2002 Report Research Report. Retrieved July 24, 2007, from http://www.aarp.org/research/family/grandparenting/aresearch-import-481.html

Davis, T., & Osborn, C. (2000). *The solution-focused school counselor: Shaping professional practice.* Philadelphia, PA: Accelerated Development.

de Shazer, S. (1988). *Clues: Investigating solutions in brief therapy.* New York: W. W. Norton.

De Jong, P., & Berg, I. (2001). *Instructor's resource manual of interviewing for solutions.* New York: Brooks/Cole.

De Jong, P., & Berg, I. (2002). *Interviewing for solutions* (2nd ed.). New York: Brooks/Cole.

De Jong, P., & Berg, I. (2008). *Interviewing for solutions* (2nd ed.) Belmont, CA: Brooks/Cole-Thomson Learning.

De Jong, P., & Hopwood, L. E. (1996). Outcome research on treatment conducted at the Brief Family Therapy Center, 1992 1993. In S. D. Miller, M. A. Hubble, & B. L. Duncan (Eds.), *Handbook of solution-focused brief therapy* (pp. 272–298). San Francisco: Jossey Bass.

De Jong, P., & Miller, S. D. (1995). How to interview for client strengths. *Social Work, 40*(6), 729–736.

Delpit, L., & Kohl, H. (2006). *Other people's children: Cultural conflict in the classroom* (2nd ed.). New York: New Press.

Duncan, B., Hubble, M., & Miller, S. (Eds.). (1999). *Heart and soul of change: What works in therapy.* Washington, DC: American Psychological Association Press.

Duncan, B. L., Miller, S. D., & Sparks, J. (2004). *The heroic client: A radical way to improve effectiveness through client-directed, outcome informed therapy.* San Francisco: Jossey-Bass.

Dupper, D. (2006). Guides for designing for designing and establishing alternative school programs for dropout. In C. Franklin, M. B. Harris, & P. Allen-Meares (Eds.), *The school services sourcebook: A guide for school-based professionals* (pp. 413–422). New York: Oxford University Press.

Eakes, G., Walsh, S., Markowksi, M., Cain, H., & Swanson, M. (1997). Family centered brief solution-focused therapy with chronic schizophrenia: A pilot study. *Journal of Family Therapy, 19,* 145–158.

Epstein, M. H., & Sharma, J. M. (2004). *BERS-2 examiner's manual.* Austin, TX: Pro-Ed.

Evertson, C. M., & Weinstein, C. S. (2006). *Handbook of classroom management: Research, practice, and contemporary issues* (pp. viii, 73–95, 1346 pp). Mahwah, NJ: Lawrence Erlbaum Associates Publishers.

Ferguson, R. (October 21, 2002). What doesn't meet the eye: Understanding and addressing racial disparities in high-achieving suburban schools from The Tripod Project Background. Retrieved August 1, 2007, from http://www.tripodproject.org/uploads/file/What_doesnt_meet_the_eye.pdf

Fong, R. (2004). Immigrant and refugee children and families. In R. Fong (Ed.), *Culturally competent social work practice with immigrant children and families.* New York: Guilford Press.

Franklin, C. (2006). The future of school social work practice: Current trends and opportunities. *Advances in Social Work, 6*(1), 167–181.

Franklin, C. (2007). Teaching evidence-based practices: Strategies for implementation: A response to Mullen et al. and Proctor. *Research on Social Work Practice, 17*(9), 592–602.

Franklin, C., Biever, J., Moore, K., Clemons, D., & Scamardo, M. (2001). The effectiveness of solution-focused therapy with children in a school setting. *Research on Social Work Practice, 11*(4), 411–434.

Franklin, C., Corcoran, J., Nowicki, J., & Streeter, C. (1997). Using client self-anchored scales to measure outcomes in solution-focused brief therapy. *Journal of Systemic Therapies, 10*(3), 246–265.

Franklin, C., Harris, M. B., & Allen-Meares, P. (2006). *The School Services Sourcebook: A guide for school-based professionals.* New York: Oxford University Press.

Franklin, C., & Hopson, L. M. (2004). Into the schools with evidence-based practices. *Children & Schools, 26*(2), 67–70.

Franklin, C., & Hopson, L. M. (2007). Facilitating the use of evidence-based practices in community organizations. *The Journal of Social Work Education. 43*(3), 1–28

Franklin, C., & Streeter, C. L. (2004). *Solution-focused accountability schools for the 21st century.* Austin, TX: The Hogg Foundation for Mental Health, The University of Texas at Austin.

Franklin, C., Moore, K., & Hopson, L.M. (2008). Effectiveness of solution-focused brief therapy in a school setting. *Children & Schools, 30*, 15–26.

Franklin, C., Streeter, C. L., Kim, J. S., & Tripodi, S. J. (2007). The effectiveness of a solution-focused, public alternative school for dropout prevention and retrieval. *Children & Schools, 29*, 133–144.

Fuller-Thomson, E., & Minkler, M. (2000). African American grandparents raising grandchildren: A national profile of demographic and health characteristics. *Health and Social Work, 25*, 109–118.

Gambrill, E. (1999). Evidence-based practice: An alternative to authority-based practice. *Families in Society: The Journal of Contemporary Human Services, 80*(4), 341–350.

Garner J. (2004). Creating solution-building schools training program. In C. Franklin, & C.L. Streeter (Eds.), *Solution-Focused accountability schools for the 21st century.* Austin, TX: The Hogg Foundation for Mental Health, The University of Texas at Austin.

Garza High School. (2006). Garza High School Annual Report. Retrieved August 9, 2007, from http://www.austinschools.org/campus/garza/documents/Garza%20HS%20AnnualReport05–06.pdf

Geil, M. (1998). Solution-focused consultation: An alternative consultation model to manage student behavior and improve classroom environment. Unpublished doctoral dissertation. University of Northern Colorado, Greely, CO.

Gingerich, W., & Eisengart, S. (2000). Solution-focused brief therapy: A review of outcome research. *Family Process, 39*(4), 477–496.

Glass, G. V. (1976). Primary, secondary, and meta-analysis. *Educational Researcher, 5,* 3–8.

Gleason, E. (2007). A strength-based approach to the social developmental study. *Children & Schools, 29*(1), 51–59.

Goldman, H. H., & Azrin, S. T. (2003). Public policy and evidence-based practice. *Psychiatric Clinics of North America, 26,* 899–917.

Goldman, H. H., Ganju, V., Drake, R. E., Gorman, P., Hogan, M., Hyde, P. S., et al. (2001). Policy implications for implementing evidence-based practices. *Psychiatric Services, 52*(12), 1591–1597.

Gorey, K. M. (1996). Effectiveness of social work intervention research: Internal versus external evaluations. *Social Work, 7*(2), 63–80.

Gorey, K. M., Thyer, B. A., & Pawluck, D. E. (1998). Differential effectiveness of prevalent social work practice models: A meta-analysis. *Social Work, 47*(3), 269–278.

Greene, R. (Ed.) (2007). *Risk and resiliency in social work practice* (p. 124). Belmont, CA: Brooks/Cole Johnny.

Gutkin, T. B., & Curtis, M. J. (1999). School-based consultation theory and practice: The art and science of indirect service delivery. In C. R. Reynolds & T. B. Gutkin (Eds.), *The handbook of school psychology* (3rd ed., pp. 598–637). New York: John Wiley & Sons, Inc.

Hall, J. A., Tickle-Degnen, L., Rosenthal, R., & Mosteller, F. (1994). Hypotheses and problems in research synthesis. In H. Cooper & L. V. Hedges (Eds.), *The Handbook of research synthesis* (pp. 17–28). New York: Russell Sage Foundation.

Hammond, C., & Reimer, M. (2006). Essential elements of quality after-school programs. Retrieved July 15, 2007, from http://www.cisnet.org/working_together/after-school.asp

Hawley, K. M., & Weisz, J. R. (2002). Increasing the relevance of evidence-based treatment review to practitioners and consumers. *Clinical Psychology: Science and Practice, 9,* 225–230.

Herie, M., & Martin, G. W. (2002). Knowledge diffusion in social work: A new approach to bridging the gap. *Social Work, 47*(1), 85–95.

Hoagwood, K. (2003). Evidence-based practices in child and adolescent mental health: Its meaning, application, and limitations. *NAMI Beginnings, Fall Issue*(3), 3–7.

House, A. (2002). *DSM-IV diagnosis in the schools.* New York: Guilford.

Howard, M. O., McMillen, C. J., & Pollio, D. E. (2003). Teaching evidence-based practice: Toward a new paradigm for social work education. *Research on Social Work Practice, 13*(2), 234–259.

Huang, M. (2001). A comparison of three approaches to reduce marital problems and symptoms of depression. Unpublished Dissertation. University of Florida.

Jensen, P. S., Hoagwood, K., & Trickett, E. J. (1999). Ivory towers or earthen trenches? Community collaborations to foster real-world research. *Applied Developmental Science, 3*(4), 206–213.

Jordan, W. J., Lara, J., & McPartland, J. M. (1996). Exploring the causes of early dropout among race-ethnic and gender groups. *Youth & Society, 28*(1), 62.

Kazdin, E. (2005). Treatment outcomes, common factors, and continued neglect of mechanisms of change. *Clinical Psychology: Science and Practice, 12*(2), 184–188.

Kelly, M., & Bluestone-Miller, R. (2007). Manuscript under review.

Kim, J. S. (2008). Examining the effectiveness of solution-focused brief therapy: A meta-analysis. *Research on Social Work Practice.*

Kiser, D. (1988). A follow-up study conducted at the brief family therapy center. Unpublished manuscript.

LaFountain, R. M., & Garner, N. E. (1996). Solution-focused counseling groups: The results are in. *Journal for Specialists in Group Work, 21*(2), 128–143.

Lambert, M. J. (2005). Early response in psychotherapy: Further evidence for the importance of common factors rather than placebo effects. *Journal of Clinical Psychology, 6*(1), 855–869.

Lambert, M. J., Hansen, N. B., & Finch, A. E. (2001). Client-focused research: Using client outcome data to enhance treatment effects. *Journal of Consulting and Clinical Psychology, 69,* 159–172.

Lambert, M. J., Okiishi, J. C., Finch, A. E., & Johnson, L. D. (1998). Outcome assessment: From conceptualization to implementation. *Professional Psychology: Research and Practice, 29*(1), 63–70.

Lever, N., Anthony, L., Stephan, S., Moore, E., Harrison, B., & Weist, M. (2006). Best practice in expanded school mental health services. In C. Franklin, M. Harris, & P. Allen-Meares (Eds.), *School services sourcebook* (pp. 1011–1020). New York: Oxford Press.

Lindforss, L., & Magnusson, D. (1997). Solution-focused therapy in prison. *Contemporary Family Therapy, 19,* 89–103.

Lipchik, E. (2002). *Beyond technique in solution-focused therapy.* New York: The Guilford Press.

Littrell, J. M., Malia, J. A., & Vanderwood, M. (1995). Single-session brief counseling in a high school. *Journal of Counseling and Development, 73,* 451–458.

Loesel, F., & Koeferl, P. (1987). Evaluation research on the social-therapeutic prison: A meta-analysis. *Gruppendynamik, 18,* 385–406.

Lipchik, E. (1994). The rush to be brief. *Family Therapy Networker, 18*(2), 35–39.

Littrell, J. M., Malia, J. A., & Vanderwood, M. (1995). Single-session brief counseling in a high school. *Journal of Counseling and Development, 73,* 451–458.

Macdonald, A. J. (2007). *Solution-focused therapy: Theory, research and practice.* London: Sage Books.

Marinaccio, B. C. (2001). The effects of school-based family therapy. Unpublished Dissertation. University of New York at Buffalo.

Marzano, R. J. (2003). *What works in schools: Translating research into action.* Alexandria, VA: Association for Supervision and Curriculum Development.

McGoldrick, M., Giordano, J., & Pearse, J. K. (1996). *Ethnicity and family therapy* (2nd ed.). New York: Guilford Press.

Mendez-Morse, S. (1992). Leadership characteristics that facilitate school change. Southwest Educational Development Laboratory Report. Retrieved May 10, 2002, from http://www.sedl.org/pubs/catalog/items/cha02.html

Metcalf, L. (1995). *Counseling towards solutions: A practical solution-focused program for working with students, teachers, and parents.* New York: Jossey-Bass.

Miller, G., & de Shazer, S. (2000). Emotions in solution-focused therapy: A re-examination. *Family Process, 39*(1), 5–23.

Moskowitz, E. (2001). *In therapy we trust: America's obsession with self-fulfillment.* Baltimore: Johns Hopkins Press.

Murphy, J. (1996). Solution-focused brief therapy in the school. In S. Miller, M. Hubble, & B. Duncan (Eds.), *Handbook of solution-focused brief therapy* (pp. 184–204). San Francisco: Jossey-Bass Publishers.

Murphy, J. J. (1997). *Solution-focused counseling in middle and high schools.* Alexandria, VA: American Counseling Association.

Murphy, J. J., & Duncan, B. L. (2007). *Brief intervention for school problems* (2nd ed.). New York: Guilford.

Myers, L. L., & Thyer, B. A. (1997). Should social work clients have the right to effective treatment? *Social Work, 42*(3), 288–299.

National Education Association. (2007). Attracting and keeping quality teachers. Retrieved August 4, 2007, from http://www.nea.org/teachershortage/index.html

Newsome, S. (2004). Solution-focused brief therapy (SFBT) group work with at-risk junior high school students: Enhancing the bottom-line. *Research on Social Work Practice, 14*(5), 336–343.

Newsome, S. (2005). The impact of solution-focused brief therapy with at-risk junior high school students. *Children & Schools, 27*(2), 83–90.

Newsome, W. S., & Kelly, M. (2004). Grandparents raising grandchildren: A solution-focused brief therapy approach in school settings. *Social Work with Groups, 27*(4), 65–84.

Norcross, J., & Goldried, M. (2003). *Handbook of psychotherapy integration.* New York: Oxford Press.

Norcross, J., & Prochaska, J. (2002). Using the stages of change. *Harvard Mental Health Letter, 18,* 3–5.

Norris, J. A. (2003). Looking at classroom management through a social and emotional learning lens. *Theory Into Practice, 42*(4), 313–318.

Nylund, D., & Corsiglia, V. (1994). Becoming solution-focused forced in brief therapy: Remembering something important we already knew. *Journal of Systemic Therapies, 13*(1), 5–12.

O'Hanlon, B., & Bertolino, B. (1998). *Even from a broken web: Brief, respectful solution-oriented therapy for sexual abuse and trauma.* New York: Wiley.

O'Hanlon, J., & Clifton, D. (2004). *Effective principals: Positive principles at work.* New York: Rowman & Littlefield.

Overholser, J.C. (1993). Elements of the Socratic method: I. systematic questioning. *Psychotherapy, 30,* 67–74.

Peterson, C., & Seligman, M. E. P. (2004). *Character strengths and virtues: A classification and handbook.* New York: Oxford University Press.

Polk, G. W. (1996). Treatment of problem drinking behavior using solution-focused therapy: A single subject design. *Crisis Intervention, 3,* 13–24.

Pollock, R., & Kuo, I. (2004). Treatment of anxiety disorders: an update. *Medscape International Congress of Biological Psychiatry Highlights of the International Congress of Biological Psychiatry,* 22–40.

Raines, J. C. (2004). Evidence-based practice in school social work: A process in perspective. *Children & Schools, 26*(2), 71–86.

Raines, J. C. (2008). *Evidence-based practice in school-based mental health: A primer for school social workers, psychologists, and counselors.* New York: Oxford University Press.

Reamer, M. S., & Cash, T. (2003). *Alternative schools: Best practices for development and education.* Clemson, SC: National Dropout Prevention Center/Network.

Reid, W. J. (2002). Knowledge for direct social work practice: An analysis of trend. *Social Service Review, 770*(1), 6–33.

Reisner, A. D. (2005). Common factors, empirically validated treatments, and recovery models of therapeutic change. *The Psychological Record, 55*, 377–399.

Responsive Classroom. (2006). Social and Academic Learning Study (SALS). Retrieved August 1, 2007, from http://www.responsiveclassroom.org/research/index.html

Reynolds, D. (2001). *Effective school leadership: The contributions of school effectiveness research*. Retrieved May 10, 2002, from http://www.ncsl.org.uk/index.cfm?pageid=ev_auth_reynolds

Roehrig, A., Presley, M., & Talotta, D. (2002). *Stories of beginning teachers: First-year challenges and beyond*. South Bend, IN: Notre Dame Press.

Rubin, A., & Parrish, D. (2007). Challenges to the future of evidence-based practice in social work education. *Journal of Social Work Education, 43*, 405–428

Rumberger, R. W., & Thomas, S. L. (2000). The distribution of dropout and turnover rates among urban and suburban high school. *Sociology of Education, 79*(1), 39–67.

Sackett, D. L., Straus, S. E., Richardson, W. S., Rosenberg, W., & Haynes, R. B. (2000). *Evidence-based medicine: How to practice and teach EBM*. Edinburg: Churchill Livingston.

Saleebey, D. (1992). *The strengths perspective in social work practice*. New York: Longman.

Seagram, B. M. C. (1997). The efficacy of solution-focused therapy with young offenders. Unpublished dissertation. York University (Canada).

Selekman, M. (2005). *Pathways to change* (2nd ed.). New York: Guilford.

Sklare, G. (1997). *Brief counseling that works: A solution-focused approach for school counselors*. Thousand Oaks, CA: Sage.

Solution-Focused Brief Therapy Association (2006). SFBT Training Manual. Retrieved July 3, 2007, from http://www.sfbta.org/

Southam-Gerow, M. A., Weisz, J. R., & Kendall, P. C. (2003). Youth with anxiety disorders in research and service clinics: Examining client differences and similarities. *Journal of Clinical Child and Adolescent Psychology, 32*(3), 375–385.

Springer, D. W., & Franklin, C. (2003). Standardized assessment measures and computer assisted assessment technologies. In C. Jordan & C. Franklin (Eds.), *Clinical assessment for social workers: Quantitative and qualitative methods* (pp. 97–138). Chicago: Lyceum Press.

Springer, D. W., Lynch, C., & Rubin, A. (2000). Effects of a solution-focused mutual aid group for Hispanic children of incarcerated parents. *Child & Adolescent Social Work Journal, 17*(6), 431–432.

Stalker, C., Levene, J., & Coady, N. (1999). Solution-focused brief therapy—One model fits all? *Families in Society, 80*(5), 468–477.

Streeter C.L. & Franklin, C. (2002). Standards for school social work in the 21st century. In Albert Roberts & Gilbert Greene (Eds.). *Social worker's desk reference.* New York: Oxford University Press.

Stricker, G. (2003). Evidence-based practice: The wave of the past. *The Counseling Psychologist, 31*(5), 546–554.

Sundman, P. (1997). Solution-focused ideas in social work. *Journal of Family Therapy, 19,* 159–172.

Sundstrom, S. M. (1993). Single-session psychotherapy for depression: Is it better to be problem-focused or solution-focused? Unpublished dissertation. Iowa State University.

Tallman, K., & Bohart, A. (1999). The client as a common factor: Clients as self-healers. In B. Duncan, M. Hubble, & S. Miller (Eds.), *The heart and soul of change: What works in therapy* (pp. 91–132). Washington, DC: American Psychological Association Press.

Texas Education Agency. (2006). 2006 campus accountability data table: Alternative education accountability procedures. Retrieved August 8, 2007, from http://www.austinschools.org/campus/garza/documents/Campus%20Accountability%202006.pdf

Thomas, F. N. (1997). What you see is what you get: Competency-based techniques with couples, families, and other earth units. Paper presented at the Texas Network for Children.

Triantafillou, N. (1997). A solution-focused approach to mental health supervision. *Journal of Systemic Therapies, 16*(4), 305–328.

Triantafillou, N. (2002). Solution-focused parent groups: A new approach to the treatment of youth disruptive behavior. Unpublished Dissertation. University of Toronto.

Tripod Project. (2007). Background of Tripod research project. Retrieved August 1, 2007, from http://www.tripodproject.org/index.php/about/about_background/

Van Heusden, H. S. (2000). *Comprehensive school reform: Research strategies to achieve high standards.* San Francisco: WestEd.

Wampold, B. E. (2001). *The great psychotherapy debate: Models, methods and findings.* Mahwah, NJ: Erlbaum.

Watkins, A. M., & Kurtz, P. D. (2001). Using solution-focused intervention to address African American male overrepresentation in special education: A case study. *Children & Schools, 23,* 223–235.

Waxman, H. C., Anderson, L., Huang, S. L., & Weinstein, T. (1997). Classroom process differences in inner city elementary schools. *The Journal of Educational Research, 91*(1), 49–59.

Weisz, J. R. (2004). *Psychotherapy for children and adolescents: Evidence-based treatments and case examples.* Cambridge: Cambridge University Press.

Weisz, J. R., Chu, B. C., & Polo, A. J. (2004). Treatment dissemination and evidence-based practice: Strengthening intervention through clinician-researcher collaboration. *Clinical Psychology: Science and Practice, 11,* 300–307.

Weisz, J. R., McCarty, C. A., & Valeri, S. M. (2006). Effects of psychotherapy for depression in children and adolescents: A meta-analysis. *Psychological Bulletin, 132*(1), 132–149.

Weisz, J. R., Weiss, B., Han, S. S., Granger, D. A., & Morton, T. (1995). Effects of psychotherapy with children and adolescents revisited: A meta-analysis of treatment outcome studies. *Psychological Bulletin, 117,* 450–468.

Wentzel, K.R. (1991). Social Competence at School: Relation between Social Responsibility and Academic Achievement. *Review of Educational Research, 61*(1), 1–24.

Wing Sue, D., & McGoldrick, M. (2005). *Multicultural social work practice.* New York: Wiley.

Wylie, M. (1994, March/April). *Endangered species.* Family Therapy Networker.

Zimmerman, T. S., Jacobsen, R. B., MacIntyre, M., & Watson, C. (1996). Solution-focused parenting groups: An empirical study. *Journal of Systemic Therapies, 15,* 12–25.

Zimmerman, T. S., Prest, L. A., & Wetzel, B. E. (1997). Solution-focused couples therapy groups: An empirical study. *Journal of Family Therapy, 19*(2), 125–144.

Index

Note: Page numbers in *italics* refer to figures, tables and boxes.